1999text

A LEAP OF FAITH:
THE CALL TO ART

ABOUT THE AUTHOR

Ellen G. Horovitz, Ph.D., A.T.R., B.C., is Director of Graduate Art Therapy at Nazareth College, in Rochester, New York and currently‐serves as Education Chair of the American Art Therapy Association. Dr. Horovitz has worked for over twenty-five years as an art therapist with myriad populations. She is currently in private practice and specializes in family art therapy with the deaf. Dr. Horovitz has received numerous awards including the prestigious 1999 "Excellence in Teaching Award" at Nazareth College. She has also published numerous articles and book chapters and authored *Spiritual Art Therapy: An Alternate Path (1994)*. (Proceeds from the aforementioned book go to the Horovitz Scholarship, established at Nazareth College to benefit students in her graduate art therapy program.) Besides being an avid painter, sculptor, and writer, she is mother to Kaitlyn and Bryan Darby.

A LEAP OF FAITH

The Call to Art

By

ELLEN G. HOROVITZ, Ph.D., A.T.R., B.C.

With a Foreword by

Valerie Appleton, Ed.D., A.T.R., M.F.C.C., N.C.C.

Charles C Thomas
PUBLISHER • LTD.
SPRINGFIELD • ILLINOIS • U.S.A.

Published and Distributed Throughout the World by

CHARLES C THOMAS • PUBLISHER, LTD.

2600 South First Street
Springfield, Illinois 62704

© *1999 by* CHARLES C THOMAS • PUBLISHER, LTD.

ISBN 0-398-07001-6 (cloth)
ISBN 0-398-07002-4 (paper)

Library of Congress Catalog Card Number: 99-37850

With THOMAS BOOKS *careful attention is given to all details of manufacturing
and design. It is the Publisher's desire to present books that are satisfactory as to their
physical qualities and artistic possibilities and appropriate for their particular use.*
THOMAS BOOKS *will be true to those laws of quality that assure a good name
and good will.*

Printed in the United States of America
TH-R-3

Library of Congress Cataloging-in-Publication Data

Horovitz, Ellen G.
    A leap of faith: the call to art / by Ellen G. Horovitz; with a
foreword by Valerie Appleton.
        p.   cm.
    Includes bibliographical references and index.
    ISBN 0-398-07001-6 (cloth). -- ISBN 0-398-07002-4 (pbk)
    1. Existential psychotherapy Case studies. 2. Psychotherapy-
-Religous aspects Case studies. 3. Art therapy Case studies.
I. Title.
RC489.E93H667   1999
616.89'14--dc21   99-37850
                                                                   CIP

This book is dedicated to my sister, Nancy Bachrach, President of the defunct Toes Club, and my two wonderful children, Kaitlyn Leah Darby and Bryan James Darby.

FOREWORD

In any profession, brave authors are needed to write about paradigm shifts. As Hillman revisioned psychology by analyzing it, Ellen Horovitz examines art therapy in a method that is true to art therapy. In her new book *A Leap of Faith, The Call to Art*, she examines the diverse and convergent roles of the therapist as artist, and artist as therapist.

As a member of Ellen Horovitz' doctoral committee I was interviewed for this volume. Her questions about art making, healing, and transcendence caused me to reflect on my own professional life in sometimes disturbing but rich ways. What had changed in my art while working on a burn unit for 13 years? Did I ever forfeit parts of my identity as artist or art therapist, while acquiring advanced titles? Can I share professionally what I learned personally from my art and professional life? As in this book, I have found the journey taken with Ellen Horovitz to be an affirming one.

With her groundbreaking text, *Spiritual Art Therapy: An Alternate Path* (1994), Ellen Horovitz asked art therapy to enlarge its definition of practice. Though not intended as a sequel to the original treatise on spirituality, this new book engages spiritual and values questions in an effort to define what is essential in art therapy. In *A Leap to Faith, The Call to Art*, we return to the primacy of art in her life. This return to art, or the "call to art," changed her identity and efficacy as a therapist. We see artwork, fiction, and clinical work change as insight occurs. She states:

> Since returning to studio my therapeutic interventions have changed considerably. I have been transformed and in the process my work has also transmuted. We engaged in rather unconventional practices in the name of "human art." We became art.

The casework throughout the book provides models for integrating the assessment and intuitive features of art therapy practice. Drawn from over 15 years of research and clinical work at Hillside Children Center and as an art therapy educator, her work is shared without guile. For example, in the poignant case of Brian, the honesty and synchronicities of the story provide moving examples of change for both the patient and therapist. We see how exploring new directions offered her better answers from the initial assessment measures, through the art therapy process, and visits with the client years later. As is typical of Ellen Horovitz' writing, the case reminds us to be aware of quality control in our profession. She demonstrates how to discover if art therapy works—by asking the patient.

Spirituality links across this treatise through an interesting syllogism. The fundamental process of art making that guides personal and professional life is described as *"elemental play."* Play is seen as the intrinsic element of the art making process that offers directions for resolution of conflicts, the evolution of personal growth, and ultimately *"soulution."* This concept of *"soulution"* is fundamental to her thesis, that art offers the necessary elements of healing. In this way the spiritual dimension of her work shines through. I do not believe she would ever separate it. For Ellen Horovitz, the leap to understanding requires faith. Faith, or the suspension of disbelief, leads the author to an understanding of the creative state. The creative state is further likened to the diagnostic category of depersonalization. However, rather than being a pathologic state, Ellen Horovitz describes the process of creative immersion as a healthy dissociative state. Further, she suggests the thought-provoking concept that individuation is a by-product of this dissociative condition.

During a time of capitated services and pressures for changes in our professional roles, a return to the studio may be a leap of faith for many in clinical work. However, this book offers a timely perspective for the art therapy profession. Reading it, we are left with a deeper sense of purpose and identity, both as artists and as art therapists. Ellen Horovitz makes a call to art, for the novice and for the seasoned art therapist that will prove to be provocative and fulfilling. For any reader, whether trained in art therapy or not, it validates the transcendent aspects of art, creativity, and play. In these ways, it affirms what is numinous and as she suggests, sacred about art.

Valerie Appleton, Ed.D., A.T.R., M.F.C.C., N.C.C.
Associate Professor/Director
Eastern Washington University
Spokane, Washington

ACKNOWLEDGMENTS

There are many people that I wish to thank regarding the fruition of this work. Primarily, I have to thank my patients and my students for all that they have taught me and continue to teach me. Specifically, I am grateful to my family, namely, my "siesta," Nancy Bachrach; my brother, Len Horovitz, M.D.; my sister-in-law, Valerie Jean Saalbach; Orin Wechsberg, my brother-in-law; my mother, Maida Pearl Horovitz; my "other" mother, Carol Darby; and, of course, my children, Kaitlyn Leah and Bryan James Darby. I could never have completed this work without the assistance of my dear friends, Laurie and Bruce Konte, nor without the support of Darlene Esposito, A.T.R. and Victoria Laneri, A.T.R. Moreover, I would like to name a number of people who supported this work in myriad ways through conversation and contributions: Parker Palmer, Dr. John Domini, Dr. David Henley, Dr. Shaun McNiff; Dr. Bruce Moon, Cathy Moon, Lynn Kapitan, Dr. Valerie Appleton, Ai Gvdhi Waya (aka Dr. Eileen Nauman), Sandy Mitzner, M.D., Charlene Goldblatt, Holly Feen-Calligan, Ron Netsky, Dr. Dennis Silva, Dr. Kay Marshman, Gail Bellamy, Gaetano Giordano, M.D., John Woodcock, Dr. Robert Burdette Sweet, Dr. Stanford Searl, Elizabeth Gray, Lori Wuest, Dr. Andrew Stein, and 'Doc' Marshall DeMotte Gates III. As well, I want to thank Rowe Photographic who helped me with the images for this text, specifically, Steve Bolton and Brandon Vick. Finally, I wish to thank Union Institute for helping me hold the "process" near and dear and specifically Dr. Carol Barrett, who made me "dare to dream."

CONTENTS

A LEAP OF FAITH: THE CALL TO ART

For there are dark streams in this dark world, lady, Gulf Streams and Arctic currents of the soul.

CONRAD AIKEN, PRELUDES FOR MEMNON

INTRODUCTION: PRIMING THE PUMP

Mourning, Loss, Soulution, and the Studio

The studio. That word alone reminds me of my senses. As a creative human being, the idea of the studio is analogous to the crisp sound of leaves crunching beneath my feet, the salt smell of the ocean as the waves lick the sandy shore, the feel of silky wet clay as it rises in my hands on a potter's wheel. In short, making art —being art connects me to my most primal senses, my healthy self.

I believe that when looking at the etiology of dis-ease, focusing on mourning and loss issues *must* be the principal step towards recovery (Horovitz-Darby, 1994). Without this primacy, there may be change but not resolution, evolution or *soulution. Soulution* evokes the concept of wedding a humanistic approach to one's work and operating from the heart. If one truly functions from this center, one cannot help being both authentic and demanding the same from others.

In this book, I operate from the aforementioned position as well as suggest a return to the studio, not just for myself but also for my patients and students. I demonstrate how very elemental this creative drive runs in our innermost psyche. But here the term "studio" requires definition. There are many that romanticize the studio, viewing it perhaps as an elitist sanctuary where the artist retreats to compose "great works of arts," masters if you will. Few artists or art therapists for that matter may have the conditions just described. Instead, they may work in a corner of a room. While most artists long for more elaborate surroundings, the maxim, "home is where you hang your hat," may be applicable here. That is, the studio need not be fancy but instead offer a refuge to practice creative thinking. Essential ingredients for such space imply growth, discovery, and risk-taking.

While the studio space may offer an outlet for such joyous productivity, oftentimes, the art does not. The art can be riddled with a litany of unwanted guests, each clawing to get out and be received. Like the facets of dissociative identity disorder (DID), the artistic temperament can be split asunder and the artwork may reflect such confusion. Nevertheless, this labyrinth may eventually wend its pathway toward a more integrated whole and produce salubrious results. While the work can be harrowing, the results can engender a more harmonious human being. This was my experience in "living with my art."

Living with One's Art

It is important for the reader to know that this book was an outgrowth of creating "a room of my own" (much like Virginia Woolf (1929) did in her hallmark book of similar name). And like Woolf, for me, the space truly became a sanctuary. The carryover caused me to invoke the same spirit in my clinical office. I invited patients to carve out a space for themselves and even "sign" the wall.

So the "studio," by definition, can have multifaceted meanings. But for me, it indeed became a shelter, in which I worked and even slept. This retreat was not an altogether conscious one. But, what occurred from this experience was quite a surprise to me and not at all what I had expected. The result of creating this sacred space changed my view on how to conduct therapy and perhaps how to truly "draw from within." For in living with my artwork, sleeping with my work, and then arising to my work, my foci changed and so did I. It gave me pause in thinking about the possibilities when working with my patients. The results were staggering. Indeed, it also was for me.

Chapter 1 highlights the artwork, which evolved from this sanctum, and includes my psychosocial genogram. Indeed, this resolve to carve out my own space came from the need to redefine myself. Personally, I had been going through an enormous change and my surroundings reflected this shift. Divorced and single-handedly raising my two young children caused me to redefine not only my turf but also my identity. Naturally, this introspection threw me back into therapy and my art.

I have always turned inward for solace. As a child of a manic-depressive mother, I learned to cope independently. Reliance on myself was always paramount. It had to be. Once again, as I was faced with operating solely, I longed for definition of myself as an artist, writer, mother, therapist, and above all, human being. The return to my studio was the result. My sister, Nancy Bachrach, to whom this book is dedicated, recognized this urgency. Through her generosity, I was allowed to redefine a place for myself. She offered me the money to turn my unlivable basement studio into a studio suite. She supported me in myriad ways but mostly she believed in my direction and me. When the renovation to my studio was completed (with fully tiled bath, 8 x 10 feet, that housed my Shimpo© ceramic wheel), my children remarked that I had "moved out" of the house. Indeed, in a sym-

Figure 1. The Studio Space.

bolic sense I had and by doing so I had created a "space of my own."

It was in this place that I carved out and marked my self. I worked in this space, slept in this space, and reclaimed my spirit in this hallowed refuge. What I learned from living with my art, my pain, and my preconscious psyche was that operating in this manner was very different than going to a studio to work: I lived in the studio. I slept in the studio. I danced under headphones in the studio. I wasted in the studio. I ate and drank in the studio. I was the studio. The carryover had enormous implications personally and in my work as a therapist. I was changing radically.

This change impacted every fiber of my existence. Contemporaneously, I was enrolled in a doctoral program at the Union Institute. The metamorphosis was staggering. My attitude at work changed. My interactions and relationships changed. I was mutating so quickly that even I became aware of these swings. But as I returned again and again to my art and my self, I was modeling the same for my patients and for my students. I began to note secondary gains in my patients and my students. And my students were beginning to model the same with their patients. It was like a ripple effect from a pebble cast into a great body of water.

Figure 2. The Bedroom Studio Space.

Figure 3. The Bathroom Studio Space.

Figure 4. View 2 of the Bathroom.

Beginnings

Having been schooled during the 1970s, I had the incredible privilege of being mentored by the person who (in my rather humble opinion) is the mother of Art Therapy: none other than Edith Kramer. One of the most useful messages that I received from Edith was to never forget the place of art in matters of the heart. "Ever art" Edith used to write on her communications post my graduation. And I saved those notes and have carried their importance in my work for over 20 years. As I have stated previously, (Horovitz, 1998), "Return, if you dare, to your core and in it you just might find not only the humanity of our struggle as art therapists, but the care for your own soul. May you discover a well of inspiration and ever art."

In this investigation, I offer a revisiting of art, Art Therapy and its basic principles, and to propose that the reader "revision" art much in the same way that James Hillman (1989) suggested that psychology review its purpose. Hillman proposed that therapists perforce bring all of their experiences to the therapeutic table and that while therapists struggle to invoke neutrality, we are nonetheless governed and driven by who we are and what we bring to our sessions. He stated: "Call it a program of animism, of ensouling the nonhuman, a program that would relieve the human of its self-importance. . . .Yet, the personal, so deliberately omitted, permeates every page of the book. . . . How can one truly repress the personal, since psychology is always and inescapably confession? . . . Nothing is repressed; in fact, nothing can be repressed" (1989, p. ix).

Neutrality. Time and time again, I have stated that this is a mythological position. To be neutral would by definition reject empathy. As I have stated (Horovitz-Darby, 1992): "After much soul searching, research and thought, I think I can conclude that 'analytic neutrality' is a mythological position of which I am clearly incapable. And that is because, alas, I am human. After all these years, I am painfully aware of this truth" (p. 389).

Hillman talked about "ensouling the non-human." When conjuring up such meaning, it becomes abundantly clear what he is suggesting. Struggle as we do to **not** be self-focused takes on paradoxical proportions, actually, when pondering perspective. Alas, questioning subjectivity invites philosophy into the discussion at the most primitive, basic level. And indeed, I propose to do just that in the following pages: that is, welcome a dialogue with other thinkers (Chapter 6) who have happened down this alleyway of inquiry. In fact, this is really a lifelong quest, one that has been brewing inside me for so long that it is transcending up and out. And, certainly, it is a turn about, perhaps a complete 360-degree spiraling backward from my present to my past and reeling towards my future. This inquiry examines the artwork of my patients, its import and meaning to the creator and to me as the facilitator of that process. More importantly, I explore my own reactions to my artwork both when working with patients (Chapter 2, 3, 4, and 5) as well as its influence on my own struggles to become a more empathic, authentic human being and clinician (Chapter 1).

I used to walk a stark walkabout, devoid of passion and spiritual compass. But I no longer find direction from this passageway. Instead, I seek alternative measures to "prove" my objectives. While I embrace "outcome-based measures" and believe in publishing findings that incorporate quantitative studies in order to keep the field "alive," of equal importance is the need to refuel the creative spirit, reignite passion. Like Henry James (1927), I, too, suggest that: "We work in the dark, we do what we can. Our doubt is our passion and our passion is our task. The rest is the madness of art."

It is time: time to embrace the importance of creativity, time to stop "excusing" the art in "art therapy." Many years ago, art therapy seemed adrift in a political time warp, exonerating itself from validity and often doctoring itself under a variety of titles, professions and names. In fact, many in the profession took to calling themselves "art psychotherapists." Each time I heard a colleague refer to him/herself this way, internally I cringed. That posture reminded me of an adolescent plagued with insecurities and acute acne vulgaris, constantly trying to cover up this blemish called "art therapy." It seemed the profession was attempting to prove what it was we had to offer when actually pictures ended up being "a thousand words."

Even now, over 50 years since Art Therapy's entrance as a profession, our identity still remains the key issue that splits us asunder. Of course, I understand all too well the need for such acronymic identification: historical discord amongst the earlier pioneers, insecurity, lack of political and professional status (e.g., licensing, jobs, levels of income, etc.) and self-doubt. Finally though, as we have moved into the twenty-first century, art therapy seems to have at last gained both professional standing and recognition. In fact, we have even become the subject of a fiction novel (Nykanen, 1998). In short, where I used to be greeted with "Art what?," now I find Art Therapy proliferating the culture from television sitcoms to heroines of novels. And while quantitative and qualitative methods may have contributed to that improvement, the real "outcome-based" measure, as non-verbal as it is, seems to have been generated by the key difference in what we truly have to offer: art and all of its evocative powers for investigation of self.

Unfortunately, Art Therapy has become obscured in the fields of psychology, psychoanalysis, and medicine. It has long forgotten its purpose, its place in the history of humanity and its importance. Art, once the native tongue of humankind, has lost its voice. No longer is it scribed on cave walls, echoing humanity. Instead, in recent years past, it has succumbed to media, commercialism, and lost its aesthetic compass. Sadly enough, the field of Art Therapy which once gave voice to creativity and embraced its importance, seems to have also lost sight of itself. There have been terribly few of us struggling to offer purpose, social meaning, and spiritual direction. Instead, laboratory white coats have replaced art smocks in the studios. Many others suggest taking seriously our patient's artwork as well as our own (Allen (1995a, 1995b); Moon (1996); McNiff (1992, 1995, 1998).

Quantitative research is *invaluable* to the profession of Art Therapy, its application, and its acceptance into the medical/scientific world. But I urge all art therapy clinicians, whether driven by the *vigorous inquiry* of quantitative, qualitative, heuristic, or phenomenological research to recall what first called them to this wondrous profession of ours: art. Take heart and in the teachings that first drew you to this field, summon forth your rightful place.

Truly, in order to understand other human beings and what the artwork represents for each individual, we must start with ourselves: looking within, knowing the art materials, ingesting its language and its message (Allen, 1995b; Rubin, 1984). Of equal weight is exploring one's self in therapy. The therapist who understands what it feels like to be on the hot seat experiences empathy in a completely different fashion than the clinician who has never explored this realm. Furthermore, the maxim of not being able to go any further than you have gone yourself is applicable here. This is true for therapeutic investigation as well as exploration with the art materials. Each pathway leads to self-examination and self-process. Moustakas (1994) touts heuristic research as: . . . "an approach to scientific study that employs methods and processes aimed at illuminating the nature of phenomenon and seeking its explication. . . The process is launched by questions and concerns that inspire self-awareness, self-dialogues, and self-explorations" (p. 23).

In McNiff's latest text, *Art-Based Research*, he urges the art therapist to foster studies that resonate with the researcher's experience of creative arts therapy. In other words, McNiff (1998) is suggesting that we approach research in the same creative venue that we do our own art. This is not so different than what Arnheim (1954) suggests in his research of objects. While Arnheim touts a position of relating to objects empirically, he also resonates with the concept of understanding their expressive qualities. McNiff's idea of "combining Arnheim's attentiveness to objects with Moustaka's in-depth self-examination is an altogether novel idea" (McNiff, 1998, p. 61). Furthermore, McNiff's idea of joining different elements of creative arts therapies (e.g., art, music, dance, performance, writing, etc.) dovetails with the premise behind this investigation.

Recently, I have discovered a similarity in thinking amongst art therapy researchers as well as the "paradigm shift" which seems to be afoot in our organization (Allen, 1995a, 1995b; Horovitz-Darby 1994; Moon 1996; Moon, C.; McNiff 1998). The thrust to return to our roots, our primacy, and the studio seems to have impregnated a new direction not only in practice but also in research.

Moreover, this impetus, which is instilling authenticity in creative art therapists, may give rise to a secondary gain; the influence that this direction bears on our work with our patients. What this may invoke will be viewing not only pathology but also the inherent strengths and potential for health in our patients and in our profession. And after all, isn't this where the focus should be?

Possibilities

This is an era of great change and possibility. All over the world, people are able to communicate within minutes, thanks to the Internet and technology of computers. Communication has changed dramatically since 1969 when the American Art Therapy Association established itself. AATA now has a web page, art therapy server lists (bulletin boards) abound, and as we connect into the twenty-first century, people are transmitting signals via e-mail, IRC (chat rooms), virtual reality (via video and software hookups such as CUSeeMe, IPhone, and WebPhone) and accessing and downloading information from the super highway known as the WWW (World Wide Web). The manner in which society now processes information is immediate, comprehensive, and available to anyone with a little skill and transport to a computer. While the FAQ's (frequently asked questions) are out, the facts aren't even in: electronic communication is here to stay. The unknown is its long-term impact on the user:

> The Internet remains an untamed frontier. Its rules and etiquette have evolved, and continue to evolve, from its participants. You can find unparalleled richness in human expression; the principles of mass publication are no longer the property of the elite. You can also find unconscionable mean-spiritedness, the darker side of faceless, facile communications. As a member in the electronic community, you might ask yourself how you'd like to contribute.
> *Netscape Navigator Handbook* (1995)

Yes, life has changed dramatically since the days when humankind scribed messages and drawings on caves, or has it? Actually, while technology has advanced human ability to communicate more readily and more rapidly, the manner in which human beings assimilate information has remained pretty much the same. This was profoundly articulated in a recent advertisement in the technological journal, *Wired*, May 1997. In an advertisement promoting Pentium chips by Sony Corporation was a marvelous rendition of the brain split in half. The left side, aptly dubbed the "analytical left brain" was severed from the right side, coined "creative right brain." The advertisement read: "Hard to fully experience life without the right brain." And it's true. Just search the members of AI (Artificial Intelligence) at MIT (Massachusetts Institute of Technology), and what do you come up with in that think tank? Artists, musicians and scientists. That's right. Because according to the most brilliant minds of communication such as Nicholas Negroponte (1995) of *Being Digital*, who pioneered the MIT Media lab, there is a reason for this mixture, just as there is a method to the madness of a brain which operates from both hemispheres.

Various researchers (Allen, 1995a, 1995b; Kramer, 1975; Henley, 1992; McNiff, 1992) have proven that the open studio space enhances physical relaxation, creativity and supports non-linear communication. McNiff (1995) goes so far as to suggest that we "reframe the practice of art therapy" by focusing on what the studio invokes as it effects our functioning with our patients. In this book, I have practiced just that concept and more.

The studio. The return to the studio. A hallowed place, it is. Can you recall the feelings that flutter inside you after preparing a canvas for that first daub of paint, kneading 25 pounds of clay in preparation for centering yourself and the material on the wheel, or simply tuning into your favorite music or yourself as you embark on that spiritual journey into the unknown entity where art exists?

Human communication codes, complex and mysterious, are normally based on a combination of signals that can be picked up by several senses (Chomsky, 1965). Therefore, language is not the only means of articulating thought processes. And according to Gazzaniga (1998), ". . . writing appears to be an independent system, an invention of the human species. It can stand alone and does not need to be a part of our inherited spoken language system" (p. 53).

Whenever a symbol operates there is meaning. Depictions, no less than words, are forms of symbolic expression. Since the beginning of time, art has served to communicate experiences and ideas, explicitly or implicitly, in form as well as content. Art making transcends culture, time, space, and language.

One need only open a Legos™ instruction book to see how readily art can transcend connections whether the primary language is Japanese, Ameslan, and/or English. The directions for creating the plastic forms are completely coded in visual format; that is, the instructions are presented in visual format, albeit wordless. And yet a Japanese child, a deaf child, and an American child can all sit together without sharing a spoken word and construct one of those toys. The visual format *becomes* the common thread, the unspoken language between them.

Just as the writer uses words, the artist uses the plastic elements of form, space, line, texture and color. Representation requires the review of experiences and clarification of impressions that call memory into play. Like words, visual symbols preserve ideas that might otherwise vanish. According to Silver (1970, 1976), for the "linguistically challenged," pictures appear to be a way of depicting one's knowledge base while simultaneously sharing this with others.

Many art therapists have claimed that art develops reasoning power by requiring organization and the constant exercise of judgment. Art does more than reveal emotions. By providing release from emotional tension, art has proven to be both integrating and healing (Allen, 1995a, 1995b; Henley, 1992; Horovitz-Darby, 1988, 1991, 1994; Kramer, 1975; Moon, 1990, 1996; McNiff, 1995, 1998; Naumburg, 1980; Rubin, 1984; Silver, 1970, 1976, 1989).

In unlocking the emotional playing field, art becomes purposeful and multilayered: the healing process affects every stratum of being from cognitive development to visual recall. "A picture is worth a thousand words" is not just a maxim because of the associative memories that are drawn from the recollection captured by photographic or artistic work. The memories are just the primary step. It is the secondary rung that bears the real fruit. And the secondary stair is built upon that first associative stance that is ignited by the associated image. These steps lead to avenues in the brain that are traces of memory and, in fact, can lead to further recall. For example, in working with imagery created by a sexually abused client, oftentimes the rendering leads to buried memories and triggers discourse around the trauma. The art jolts every fiber of one's collective being bridging the gap from sight to smell and from touch to sound. Perhaps this is why communication is so invisibly woven into the fabric of humankind.

In both my personal life experiences as well as in research, I have experienced these kinds of "memory." Indeed, this memory from which we operate, learn, react, and change is intrinsically wound into every fiber of our being: while most emphasize the brain and its ability to repress (yet retain) experiences and memories, so, too, does the body. Anyone who has worked in ceramic wheel throwing understands this. An analogy will serve to clarify this point.

If, when working on the potter's wheel, you remove a finished thrown piece and you are not careful in this procedure, the lip of the pot created may warp out of its originally thrown position. Every potter (in learning the formalities of wheel throwing) has discovered this. The next step on the part of the potter is to then carefully tap the piece back into its original shape. While it will dry in this newly tapped position, in the firing of the piece, oftentimes the oddest thing will occur: it will warp into the accidental position that it took when it was carelessly removed from the potter's wheel. This is referred to as the clay body "having memory." The first time I discovered this, I was astounded at the material's ability to "inherently" recall its injury. If art materials made up of less mobile atoms than a human body can have memory, think of the possibilities of the human anatomy to recall insult and injury. One need only look to the medical stories of people feeling lost limbs after amputation to begin to understand the possibility inherent in such recall.

Put in more clinical language, there are many researchers who refer to this process as "somatosynthesis." Derived from the Latin words *soma* (meaning body) and *synthesis* (meaning integration of separate elements into a unified whole) somatosynthesis is based on the concept of Robert Assagioli's work in "psychosynthesis." While Assagioli (1965) referred to the notions of healing through the mind, Clyde Ford (1992) combines the properties of both the mind and body in his proposal of healing

While I also proposed the theory of utilizing the mind, body, and spirit in my first treatise *Spiritual Art Therapy: An Alternate Path* (Horovitz-Darby,

1994), I discovered actively incorporating this belief system into assessment and treatment was a means to unlocking disease and corralling health into action. If we treat others and/or ourselves as isolated fragments, we will, indeed, lose all sense of the whole and the recovery will be only partial. When that occurs, the body/mind/spirit continuum opens itself for recurrent attack and is made vulnerable to dis-ease and serious discord.

According to Ford (1992), "tissue, from which our sense of touch arises, is uniquely capable of creating, storing, and recalling a variety of images." In fact, Ford states that "somatic tissue functions as a secondary storage facility for the brain" (p. 21). Neurochemical receptors such as neuropeptides form a communication between the brain, immune system, and our emotions. The astounding aspect of neuropeptides is their location: they are concentrated just below the skin's surface and their ability to be released through touch has led researchers to conclude that "emotions are not just in the brain...(but) in the body" (p. 22).

The Mystery of the Brain

We still know so little about the brain and the restorative powers of the mind, body, and spirit. A human story may illustrate this point. About 16 years ago, my father died and my mother was brain injured in the same accident. While she seemed normal after she came out of her coma, she declined very rapidly and within three weeks she completely deteriorated; at 54 years of age she seemed no different than an Alzheimer patient and had lost all control of her bodily functions and mental capacities. The area of her brain that had sustained the most injury was her myelin, a casing that protects the nerves and operates synaptic connections. In short, the CAT scans indicated that her myelin was completely gone and unlike other areas in the brain, it was not a cell and was incapable of regeneration. My siblings and I were informed that there was no chance of recovery.

Within time, we found her a residential placement and expected that she would live out her days in this institution. Prior to locating this residence, we had placed my mother in a hospital that touted itself on being the "best hospital in the country for brain injured patients." Every weekend I would visit her and label her drawings and read to her because she had been a writer and an avid reader. While I felt like I was relating to the wall, I needed to do this. Yet each time I would arrive there, I would discover her tied up in a gurney and she had urinated and defecated all over herself. This, I guess, was their idea of treatment. I was disgusted and appalled. I couldn't find another facility fast enough for her. But in some respects this disgusting treatment which she endured may have actually caused a regeneration of her myelin. It is difficult to say.

Some months after she entered the next residence where she lived for almost two years, she began to speak. Miraculously, she began to *read* again. While she is clearly not the same person that she was and daily restores parts of her memory that were wiped out, she is completely independent, exercises regularly, and has a remarkable social life.

When I asked her what she thought was the reason for her recovery, she recalls the "humiliation" she experienced when she was tied to that chair all day. She said it gave her the will to overcome her state. Her statement about the "humiliation" reminded me of everything that Victor Frankel talked about in his theory on logotherapy. In Frankel's (1984) poignant account of one's search for meaning, he relayed the stories of the Holocaust victims who survived because of one factor they retained that others lacked: hope.

While I will never know for certain (nor will the doctors understand) why my mother recovered, she may owe it to that horrifying and degrading experience. It gave her the will to live differently. It underscored for me (both personally and professionally) how little we know about the human spirit, mind, and body and its restorative capacities.

There is no way of ever determining why she recovered and what part of her brain stimulated this regeneration. After all, we were informed that she had no myelin and thus no clear ability to make "connections" (via the synaptic method). But one thing was clear for her; both touch (via restraint by gurneys) and language (via reading) played an integral part of her rehabilitation and communication system. Something restorative occurred for my mother through both touch and the art of language. Whether the reading sparked memory or internal pictures will remain forever unknown but both seemed to reconnect her with the world. For my mother, her inner world was linked through the imagery sparked by the books she read. The images led to restorative properties and memory.

For language is fueled by imagery. While words punctuated on the linear stage of air may occasionally fall flat, they live on in thought and sometimes deed. From this, ideas are born, enacted, and truths unfold. Cognition assembled through word serves as a springboard into imagination. Artistic imagery becomes the primal pump. It hurls us toward and reminds us of our existence in as primitive a fashion as one can imagine. Perhaps the center of synaptic connection *incorporates* this communicative ability of language and art to wed the soul to reason.

In a recent article by Michael S. Gazzaniga in *Scientific American* (July 1998), the split brain theory is revisited and the conclusions are extraordinarily different than previous research indicated. Instead of viewing the brain as operating from two distinct minds (left and right brain, respectively), the article suggests that our brains work precisely as they do because they are *not* naturally rent apart. This finding suggests that we operate in a more integrated fashion than previously had been thought. In the words of *Scientific American* editor-in-chief, John Rennie, "our homes are heads to many potential minds, not just two . . . we the uninjured enjoy the choice of finding the best or worst of those voices within us. The orators, artists, beasts and angels of our nature await us" (1998, p. 8).

While there is no empirical evidence as to why we gravitate towards artistic endeavor, the concept of culture may be closely linked to the drive to create. In a personal interview, John Woodcock (1997), a Jungian therapist specializing in sandtray work, talked about the critical element that differentiates humankind from other species: culture. He stated: "Culture is formed from the psychic act—we receive an image in the psyche and take up a relationship to that image."

Perhaps this is why we do what we do, why we make art. Just as we need to breathe, eat, sleep, waste, and yes, want, we, too, must make art. It has been and continues to be our God-given right. According to Woodcock (1997), every human being is born with this urge to create. He asserted: "Apparently the gift of specificity is that God wants to come into particularity, which is the evolutionary intentionality behind creating the ego, separating the hubris and becoming the mouthpiece of God." Some of us do this in multifaceted ways. But just as endorphins cry out daily for their regimental workout, somewhere, deep in the recesses of that right temporal lobe, comes a far and distant cry imprinted by the ancestors of humanity. It bellows loudly until it is heard, understood, and allowed entrance repeatedly to that sole purpose.

So why do we make art? For me, the answer goes way beyond "because I have to." This book's aim is to explore that question and its connection to language, cognition, and thought processes. This is an inquiry about art and its capacity to inform the self. This is not about self focus. In contrast, this is about the human quest of self, community, and the incessant search for meaning. Such passage tills the final frontier: becoming a more authentic person and therapist. But there is more. There is a secondary gain in how this will impact the people whom you so earnestly hope to serve: your patients and self.

Content Descriptions

Chapter 1 explores creativity and its ability to fuel inquiry and growth. Emphasis is placed on personal accounts of my artwork and its outgrowth in terms of introspection, insight, and change. My artwork and self-analysis is highlighted as I invite the reader to research similar themes in activating self-inquiry and transformation. In describing that experience to the reader, a fictional short story fueled by the creative art process, illustrates how the visual arts can influence the literal arts and inform cognition and recovery in the human spirit.

In Chapter 2, the reader is asked to look at how an artist approaches his/her artwork and connect that same teaching principle in working with patients. Creativity, self, and psychosis are also explored as researched by various clinicians that share the hallmarks of being artists (visual, physical, musical, and or literal) and how that has impacted their lives. The fine line between creativity and madness is explored with a case vignette that reveals that discourse and questioning. Finally, the idea of the "healthy dissociative self" as a pathway towards individuation, health, and maturation is considered. A case study of a young boy troubled by the murder of his father is presented and the power of art as the healing agent is presented. Included is a rare follow-up ten years later. (Author's Note: Permission has been granted for publication of all patient work and all names have been changed to protect the identities of the clients.)

Chapter 3 illustrates primary process thinking channeled into secondary gain. The story of Brian, a misdiagnosed ten-year-old boy, is presented. Emphasis is on the treatment of this artistic boy and his eventual movement towards health via the art materials. The final section highlights Brian ten years post treatment and discusses his growth as an artist. Current interviews of Brian allow the reader to view how the art process animated his cognition, language, and self-mastery.

Chapter 4 illustrates the primary process involved in self-exploration vis-a-vis working with a multimodality approach with an adolescent client. Beyond the artwork that leads to this investigation, the old adage, "you can't take your clients any further than you have gone yourself" is given new meaning as I explore the potential of primary process work when working with clients. A solution focused, brief therapy case of an abused adolescent highlights this chapter.

Chapter 5 is a story of the almighty dragon, countertransference. It starts off with a tale that is woven around the actual work of a deaf, partially sighted patient and the issues that surfaced in my work with her. Herein the therapist is urged to explore uncharted waters in oneself and stretch into less traditional avenues in order to overcome such pitfalls in thinking.

Chapter 6 highlights interviews of writers, artists, and other creative arts therapists. In this section, I attempt to weave together the similarities and differences that summon forth the creative urges specifically in artist/writers who are drawn to work in the multifaceted ways that actually link left-brain/right-brain thinking.

In the final chapter, summaries of the issues presented in the book are reviewed and possibilities for future direction (from studio art therapy to forensic art therapy via computer application) are postulated. Moreover, the concept of creativity and the elemental surprise of art's ability to generate recovery, healing, and wellness is postulated and revisited from visual, aural, kinesthetic and literal perspectives.

Pathways

Mourning and loss issues are emphasized as the principal step towards recovery (Horovitz-Darby, 1994). I suggest that without this primacy, there may be change but not resolution, evolution or *soulution*. I recommend approaching others as I engage myself: with honor, respect, sincerity, patience, trust, and love. This is about learning to have heart, heart for those with whom we work and heart for ourselves. Walk with me as I share how art has fueled me first and foremost as a human and how this continues to inform my cognition, language, and thought as it transcends and connects me to the very fiber of my being.

Nirvana is that place where you act out of the center of yourself.
JOSEPH CAMPBELL, THE POWER OF MYTH

Chapter 1

IN SEARCH OF SELF: INFORMING THE CREATIVE PROCESS

This chapter is a rather prolonged self inquiry that is at the heart of this book. And that is: the extraordinary lengths that I have gone to investigate manic depression, creative genius, and as well, my likeness to my mother and her illness. In this section, I hope to explore the links between madness, creativity, and the continual quest for transformation via my own experiences as an artist/writer and human being.

The Road Ahead

In order to explore my artwork and its meaning, examining the history of my nuclear family is necessary. While I can already hear the musings of my colleagues as they gloat over my "airing of my dirty laundry," (that is revealing portions of my psychosocial history), I offer this information out of necessity. In fully examining my own artwork, I *must* reflect on my past (and present) and how that has driven my work, my creativity, my person, my life decisions, and in short, everything that I am. For after all, the old saying that you "can't take your patients any further than you have gone yourself" is what is applicable here. If I were to cough up ideas about a patient and his or her artwork, being the family art therapist that I am, I would consider genogram information to be pinnacle. Is it any less true when examining myself? I think not. Furthermore, when supervising incipient art therapists, I implore them to investigate their family of origin issues. Facing one's past leads not only to insight and enhanced self-understanding but also informs the therapist when contemplating the effect of transference and counter-transference issues that arise in treatment. Therefore, inspection of nodal events fuels, ignites, and potentially highlights organismic change.

A Little History

While I am prepared to reveal information about my upbringing, I would like the reader to bear in mind that the history has been somewhat "abbreviated." The reasoning is representative of a common dilemma: there are many people in my life that would be irreparably injured if I were to reveal everything that I know of my past and that of my family. So, I will reveal the most necessary of information by way of a summary herein. (see Genogram)

Ellen's Genogram and Timeline

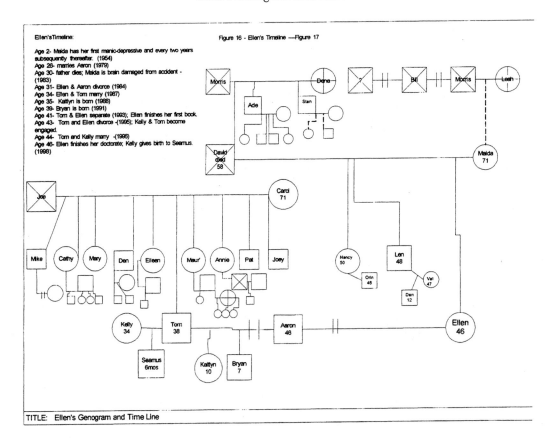

Ellen's Timeline:

Age 2- Maida has her first manic-depressive and every two years
subsequently thereafter. (1954)
Age 26- marries Aaron (1979)
Age 30- father dies; Maida is brain damaged from accident -
(1983)
Age 31- Ellen & Aaron divorce (1984)
Age 34- Ellen & Tom marry (1987)
Age 35- Kaitlyn is born (1988)
Age 39- Bryan is born (1991)
Age 41- Tom & Ellen separate (1993); Ellen finishes her first book
Age 43- Tom and Ellen divorce -(1995); Kelly & Tom become
engaged.
Age 44- Tom and Kelly marry -(1996)
Age 46- Ellen finishes her doctorate; Kelly gives birth to Seamus.
(1998)

Figure 16 - Ellen's Timeline —Figure 17

TITLE: Ellen's Genogram and Time Line

Briefly, I am 46 years old and the (now) single mother of two beautiful children (Kaitlyn, aged 10, and Bryan, aged 7). I completed my doctoral degree (while engaged in the writing of this book), and am actively involved in the education and training of students as I spearhead a graduate art therapy program.

I have two wonderful siblings, with whom I have an extremely close relationship. Nancy is 51, incredibly successful in business, and is married to a very spirited, creative, and prosperous cinematographer and director, Orin, aged 46. (Orin is also an unparalleled gardener.) Lenny is 48, a brilliant internist, surgeon and recorded concert pianist, who is married to a beautiful, bright, and talented opera singer, Valerie, aged 47. They have one very handsome and talented son named Daniel, aged 11. As seen in my description, I am very proud of my immediate family and quite frankly I am in awe of my older siblings and simultaneously proud of them and their accomplishments. I am also quite fond of their mates and we share many summers together purposely vacationing on our mutual property in the Adirondacks.

My mother, Maida, now 71 years old, was manic-depressive all of my childhood and was placed on lithium carbonate in 1969 when it became available to the general public. (I was then 17.) Prior to that, I have memories (starting at age 4) checkered by her "nervous breakdowns" (approximately every two years) and experienced a rather unstable upbringing. My father, David, a psychologically absent workaholic, armed himself with work and fixing everything mechanical as a way to avoid the ongoing, domestic chaos. He was deeply entrenched in a family-owned business with his two younger brothers (Adrian and Stanley) and father (Morris). His mother (Dena, for whom by the way, I am a dead ringer) had been hypochondriac all of my childhood. In many respects, my father had gone from a mother who needed caretaking to marrying my mother, who also demanded the same. However, when my mother would have these episodic breaks with reality, my mother's mother (Nana Leah) would take over and move in. Thanks to my rather unusual Nana (my mother's adoptive mother, but in reality her aunt), I had some stability in my life, although still not much of a role model for mothering. Nana had an equally interesting past, which she shared quite openly. She was the thirteenth child of an orthodox rabbi, had danced on the stage and cavorted with stars such as Jimmy Durante, bootlegged during the Prohibition Era, married three times, and in short, lived a rather unusual and colorful life.

Perhaps my siblings and I bonded out of necessity. Regardless, our memories of our childhood differ according to our perceptions and to this day, we compare notes. Suffice it to say, while I know it is rather unusual, my siblings and I share a rich and close relationship. Lucky me.

Growing up amongst my incredibly talented siblings (e.g., my brother represented all of New England in Music at the 1964 World's Fair, at the age of 14—no lie), was difficult at best. Being the youngest, I didn't really come into my own until I went to college. It was there that I truly allowed for my artistic prowess to flourish. When I finished graduate school, aged 26, I married Aaron, my childhood sweetheart.

Unfortunately, the marriage was an unhappy one. Five years later when my father died in an accident that also damaged my mother's brain, I decided to divorce Aaron. At my age 30, my 58-year-old father was dead and my mother, aged 54, was brain damaged, unable to control her bodily functions or recognize anyone or anything from her past. This was a very difficult time for me and for my siblings. But we all grew from this. While we were informed that our mother would "never be the same again" and for all intents and purposes would live out her days as a "gork," she fooled them. Approximately two years later, my mother's recovery began and she is now living independently; while she is definitely *not* the person of my youth, the mother I now know is docile, a tad flat on the emotional range (especially when compared to her previous manic past), and in general, much easier to be around. In short, my life changed.

Around the time of my mother's recovery period, I met my second husband. We had two fabulous children (as I indicated earlier) and we divorced after eight years of marriage. He is now remarried and has a newborn child, Seamus. Fortunately for our children, our relationship is now amicable. That is about the scope of what seems important to convey.

What seems abundantly clear to me is that I have always been looking for a mother figure. While I still seek out the ultimate mother figure, fortunately, I now know that I will never find one but oddly enough the attraction to find one is always there. And in looking at my artwork, it is clear that my need for that unconditional nurturance figure, motherhood and apple pie in the sky mentality has effected and continues to influence my artwork. It confronts me with every mark I make. While I never analyze my art work while in the process, the fragments of artistic remains reflect like shards of broken mirror frames. And I, the maker, constantly struggle to piece those jagged edges into a semblance of who I am. For as Pat Allen aptly said, "...viewing art only as a stimulus to verbal therapy sacrifices art's considerable therapeutic potential in and of its self" (1983, p. 93).

Something happens to me when I am confronted with what Don Jones called "aesthetic arrest" (1999). All of my senses become informed when I am in this state which I call "*elemental play.*" It is more than that 'ah-ha' phenomenon. It is much more primal and akin to the type of arrest one experiences from a great epic, a breathtaking image, or music that informs memory experiences. Many things trigger this response in me but when it is my own artwork that activates these warning signs, I heed their beckoning voices.

The Work

Most of my life, I have been working out my issues through my art. As an art therapist, I know this all too well. One thing I have learned in this business, though, is to never analyze myself, especially *while* engaged in the creative process. In doing so, the creative flow is literally stopped. However, well after a piece has been fabricated, it is quite easy to step back and wonder about its meaning.

Professionally, I have analyzed the work of my patients for over 20 years.

But personally, I have painted, drawn and sculpted many works of art and never had the slightest inclination and/or desire to analyze my work or even wonder about its meaning. That is, until recently.

All of my life I have walked a fine line between both the visual and literal worlds and like many artists that have gone before me, I go through "periods" where emphasis has gone either to a particular medium or mode of expression. Picasso, for example, went through his blue stage, for about a decade. And there have been decades where I have only painted in oil or worked in sculpture. While my art is no longer so definitively bordered, I still tend to go through stages where I focus on one medium at a time.

I remember in graduate school asking Edith Kramer how she switched between making art and writing. She did one or the other, never swinging back and forth between the two. Recently, at the 28th annual American Art Therapy Association conference, we dialogued again about the same point following my presentation in a poetry panel. Still, she had not wavered from this position. Since I follow the same edict for such creativity, it was affirming to hear (some twenty years later) that Edith's position remained the same. While it may differ for others, I *still* work in this fashion, that is working in concentrated fashion on one art form or the other. Even though I may have a canvas going at the same time that I am writing this chapter, the work remains connected. As I am certain that there must be some crossover pollination (that is influence from one sphere to the other), they remain separate and distinct art works. Sometimes, however, I find that the art has influenced my writing or my writing (especially my poetry) has signaled the art.

For about a month now, I have been in what I call a "writing mode." For me that consists of being consumed by the written word. Hours at a time can pass and I still sit at my laptop terminal with words flowing out as readily as paint from a tube. Akin to painting, I rework the materials until I am satisfied with the arrangement, composition, and communication. The odd part about being in this literal stage of *elemental play* is that I am completely uninterested in anything else. Eating, sleeping, exercising; nothing holds my interest except the work at hand. Naturally, when I am in a painting or sculpting mode, the same consequence occurs. Nevertheless, the distraction level is quite different. For example, I can don headphones and listen to music or even talk on the telephone (wearing a hands-free contraption) while still painting. While I prefer to do art uninterrupted, I can focus on its calling in a very different manner than when I write. For me, writing requires a very different form of concentration, one in which I must totally focus on the matter at hand. If I am interrupted from the creative state exacted during writing, it is an arduous task to return to that mode. As a result, I have discovered to write when I know that interruptions will be at a minimum. Writers such as Lamott (1995), discuss the myriad ways of focusing on such investigation: ". . . clear a space for the writing voice . . . string words together like beads that tell a story . . . you cannot will this to happen. It is a matter of persistence and faith and hard work. So you might as well go ahead and just get started" (p. 7).

Lamott (1995) goes on to talk about varied distractions and offers sound advice against such pitfalls. Her advice is both compassionate and hysterically amusing as the reader repeatedly finds him or herself in Lamott's words: "Writing can be a pretty deep endeavor, because it is about our deepest needs . . . our need to make sense of our lives, to wake up, grow, and belong . . . you can safely assume that you've created God in your own image when it turns out that God hates all the same people you do" (pp. 19-22).

But my point is that the state of *elemental play* is intuiting spiritual inquiry at its highest level. Analyzing "on an unconscious level" what this all means can stop the creative flow. It has no import when in the creative state. ***But,*** recently I have discovered that sometimes when I am in the throes of the creative process, such as when working on a painting that is deeply connected to my psyche and my issues, if I step back and try and let the image talk to me (as McNiff, [1992, 1995] so aptly suggested in his works), the imagery informs my writing and sometimes the writing informs the imagery. That is, if I allow for the dance. This two-step process remains the most informative, in-depth, self-inquiry of my psyche. It is soul work and actually akin to the process that Myss (1996) details. Let me explain.

For the past two years, I have been working (off and on) on a fiction novel that is inexactly based on growing up with my manic depressive mother. I have found that my artwork has informed my writing but lately they have informed each other, as if in a mutually creative dialogue and like Moon suggested in his pinnacle work *Art and Soul: An Artistic Psychology,* I am merely the "imageorator." For me, this has been an extremely different way of working. Part of this change has been due to in-depth exploration with my therapist, Dr. Sandra Mitzner. While I have been accustomed to sharing artwork with previous therapists, the process with Dr. Mitzner has been different, very different. And while the work has often been trying and arduous, it has been a path worth taking and one that I am still on. I have spent many years getting to the comfort level that I now have with my work, with myself, and with my art. I know that I have become a better person through this struggle and as a result, I am a better therapist. So, in essence, turning the work inward has wholesale applications. And the secondary rung bears the real fruit: if I am a better person and a better therapist, then my patients get better treatment and per force, there is a secondary gain. I pass this on to them and they also benefit and perhaps even learn from it.

Moreover, I have found this to be just as true when working with my students (or, as I like to call them, fellow learners). My role modeling an inward journey has also caused them to investigate their own imagery, be it visual, aural, kinesthetic, literal, or lyrical. The result has greatly effected student research and has resulted in serious introspection and scholarly endeavors. Call it imprinting creative health. But, I dare say, it's worth investigating.

While this might seem "elementary" and basic, perhaps it is just that: so very basic that I, in fact, missed it all these years, but no more. This reawakening to myself and my art is something that I care to share with you so perhaps you can view how it has unfolded and informed my inquiry, my thoughts, my language, my life, and my self. I speculate that while this process has been maturing for years, like a good wine, it has taken time to properly mature. Moreover, I see this journey as a continuous, lifelong quest. In fact, while the investigation has led to self-discovery, reflection and introspection, it has also resulted in more questions. Answering the often unfathomable presents new challenges, new constructs, and fresh directions. As Kodish & Kodish (1993) state, "We react to our reactions" (p. 45).

In the last 20 years, I have attempted to realistically portray the ideas and images around me. One of the ways I have always comforted myself is to fill my home with art–mine, others that I prize (including my children's magically fresh artworks), as well as artifacts from other cultures. Oftentimes, I choose to represent that which has deep and personal meaning. Such was the case in Figure 5 (see color insert), although I didn't really understand this at the time when I created it.

Originally, my intent in creating this work was quite benign and non-specific. There was a large wall over my living room couch that desperately called for a painting. I used the fabric that I had fashioned into curtains as a backdrop and set up a still life with two antique tea cups that my mother had given me. I really didn't think about the work as I meticulously fashioned it over a three-month period. I just created it. Many things about the title, which always presents itself at the work's end, were intricately woven into my novel, "*Lithium for Lunch.*" But, at the time, I was completely unaware of its deeper meaning for me. This information was not completely clear until the night of a faculty opening when I shared this work with my colleagues.

At the reception, the former Chair of the Art Department, Roger Adams, was struck by the painting (Figure 5). He thought it was splendid, quite beautiful, and indeed rather unlike my previously exhibited work. But one comment that he made struck me to the core. He simply stated, "Interesting title, especially considering that the cup is empty."

Yes, the cup was empty. While painting, many times I toyed with the idea of adding a spilled liquid–tea, milk, coffee, water, anything. But, I couldn't. At the time, I just couldn't understand it. And I really didn't understand it until that night when Roger's words resounded in my ears. A memory that I had somewhat repressed and had been writing about was illuminated by this painting. It was, in fact, about the subject that I had written. As the scene from my novel unfolds, the title of the painting will become abundantly clear:

Ellen was sitting at the Formica dining table in the puke-colored kitchen of her childhood home. The traditional dinner of canned green peas, frothy-white whipped potatoes, and flaccid-looking meatloaf dressed the everyday dinner plate, which was a reward from the local Shell gas station. Even Shell glassware was stationed at this incredibly humdrum meal. Ellen moved her fork across the plate playing with the peas. While Mother turned her back, she maneuvered a pea onto her fork and catapulted it onto Lenny's unsuspecting lap. War broke out. Suddenly, a glass of milk toppled over, running over the edges of the table.

"God damn kids!" Maida shrieked. "Now are you happy? Now are you happy? This never would have happened, David, if YOU hadn't brought that God damned carton of milk onto the table. It's positively barbaric, you know."

By now, Maida was once again on the warpath. As usual, she felt shamed by Daddy's classless qualities: he never cared about the finer things in life. In fact, he shunned them while Maida was mesmerized by their petty seductions. She lived her pretenses. Daddy, raised with money, abhorred everything about them. But Mother came from the wrong side of the tracks and it showed. The artificial flowers, decorating the urns in the entrance foyer, were a dead giveaway. They were as false and waxy as Maida herself.

She sauntered over to the toaster oven in what seemed a composed, yet thoroughly annoyed fashion. Silently, Maida removed the items one by one and arranged them on a plate. She seemed almost calm, like the sky before the storm. Everyone returned back to the business of dinner, ignoring her latest outburst.

Ellen continued to push the peas on her plate and piled them in endless design into her mashed potatoes. They were beginning to take on a pattern much like an African headdress. As usual, she became lost in her usual escape of their intricate design, her artistry.

Lenny occasionally flicked a pea across the table onto Ellen's lap. Trying to get Nancy involved in this desperate play was wasted energy. She wasn't joining. No, instead, she just turned away from Ellen and Lenny's dalliances ignoring their attempts to annoy mother further and called them "babies."

Daddy ignored Mother's protests over the spilled carton of milk, leaned back on his chair and reached behind him into the refrigerator, pulling out yet another carton. He firmly planted it onto the plastic table and looked Maida squarely in the eye. She caught his move and rather passively left the room for a period. But right before that, she shot him a look that made Ellen's insides cringe. She was furious and had reached nuclear meltdown. You could see beneath her pretentious exterior that something was bubbling up. It festered in the jerky movements that began to take over her hands as they uncontrollably shook.

A Leap of Faith

Figure 5. *Don't Cry Over Spilled Milk.* Oil on canvas, 24 x 36 inches.

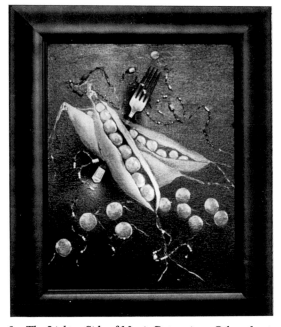

Figure 6. *The Lighter Side of Manic Depression.* Oil and mixed media

Deliberately, she walked over to the counter and grabbed a butter knife. Pensively, she twisted it back and forth, back and forth, almost methodically between her forefinger and thumb. In what seemed a religious manner, she spread butter on the Wonder bread, carefully piling up one, two, three, four, and finally five pieces of that bread. With great care, she walked them over to the table. She placed them in front of Daddy, serving him first, as she had always done.

Slowly, she walked away from the table and returned to the counter. She placed the butter dish away and then picked up the butter knife and walked briskly towards Daddy and rammed it into his unsuspecting arm.

Amazingly enough, he didn't react, not even to the pain. Ellen didn't recall him pulling the knife out or in fact doing anything at all. No instead, he picked up the milk carton and poured himself another drink. He didn't yell. He didn't scream. He didn't say anything. He just drank that milk and continued to eat his meatloaf.

Ellen was both shocked and morbidly curious. She immediately rushed out of her chair and went over to inspect Daddy's arm. His white rolled-up sleeve seemed to bear no trace of the onslaught. In fact, it seemed perfectly normal, except for the tear in the sleeve that now enclosed the shaft of the knife. Ellen lowered her eyes as much as possible in order to view the blood that she thought would be oozing out. She couldn't see anything. It all appeared so perfectly normal: Daddy calmly drinking his milk with a butter knife sticking out of his triceps, Mother pacing back and forth on the kitchen floor, Lenny staring blankly into his plate, and Nancy now perfectly paralyzed. And Ellen? What was she doing? Ellen was being the voyeur that she had become.

Finally when Daddy finished his meal, he got up from his chair and removed the handset from the telephone and called Servile Hospital. The knife still dangled from his arm. Within ten minutes, the ambulances wailed into the driveway. Mother went ballistic. Suddenly, she started screaming at the top of her lungs, "Bastard, you bastard, David!"

Lenny still sat in his seat, head now bowed into his plate. Nancy hadn't moved. She was positively catatonic. Ellen hid in the corner next to the avocado stove and watched as three men approached mother with a four-point leather restraint. Daddy seemed sullen, somewhat removed as were they all. Mother wailed uncontrollably as the first man got behind her and placed her hands behind her back. Within seconds she was flat on the kitchen floor struggling to get out from under three heaving bodies. They seemed to like this job of wrestling Mother into passivity. She fought and then almost instantly succumbed; as one of the men straddled over her head to attach the restraint from behind, she lurched forward and bit him squarely on his offshoot. He yelped, "Bitch!" and his compatriot overturned Mother and with great gusto shoved her head repeatedly onto the square dotted pattern of the linoleum floor. Once a muted tan, as Mother's mouth began to bleed, it turned a bright crimson red. They slapped some gauze on her mouth and taped her up so she couldn't wail or scream anymore.

Meanwhile, Daddy seemed oblivious ignoring the entire process. Ellen was even more sickened by the display of these three gruesome men. Then, they merely took her away.

Ellen sat there, not moving. Nancy was the first to finally recover. She stood away from her chair and instructed Ellen to start doing the dishes as she cleared the table. Without words, she handed Lenny the broom. And Daddy twisted and turned that butter knife, carefully removing the blade from his now bloodied arm. Without fanfare, he tossed that thing into the sink where Ellen was now washing the dishes. Ellen was repulsed as it splashed into the soapy water contaminating the dishes and its surroundings. The blood just oozed away from the sidewalls of the blade, meandering towards Ellen's hands in the now bloodied water. She stood over the dishwater mesmerized as the blood touched everything in its path.

Ellen couldn't move. She was transfixed and inquisitive all at the same time. Sickened by the thought of putting her hands back into that water, she spied anything that could be used to release the drain plug so that she might add new water to the sink. Meanwhile, her hands were tinged with her father's blood and she rinsed them on the other side, staring blankly at the sink and Daddy in total disbelief.

Daddy seemed undisturbed by the entire event. Calmly, he removed the garbage under the counter next to where Ellen stood and urged her to hold her fingers, still bloodied, onto the knot he was now tying around the packaged garbage. Just as she always had, she placed her finger in place and removed it when he instructed. He carried that garbage outside to the garage just as he had always done, only this time its removal seemed to have more meaning.

Ellen found a larger knife and managed to slip it underneath the drain plug finally releasing the now, pink water from the sink. The dishes, marbleized with swirls of crimson blood, revolted her. She puked on top of them and then just as casually opened up the faucet and washed the whole sordid affair down the drain.

Ellen never looked at peas quite the same way again.

I remembered that scene instantly when Roger innocently remarked about the empty teacups. While it unfolded to a more horrid place (as illustrated in the next painting), the image of the milk careening across the table and falling over the sides of the Formica table loomed in my mind more realistically than the people surrounding me at the faculty opening. My eyes then lighted on the painting that was next to it, Figure 6 (see color insert), *The Lighter Side of Manic Depression*.

Figure 6 is a very dark painting, which required approximately six months to complete. Combined, both paintings took nine months to complete. This in itself is intriguing to me. It is a multimedia painting of peas pierced with an antique silver fork from my grandmother, Nana Leah, and sewn with beads, gold embroidery, silver wire and pearls (which perhaps unconsciously represent my mother's need for the finer things in addition to her "pearls of wisdom").

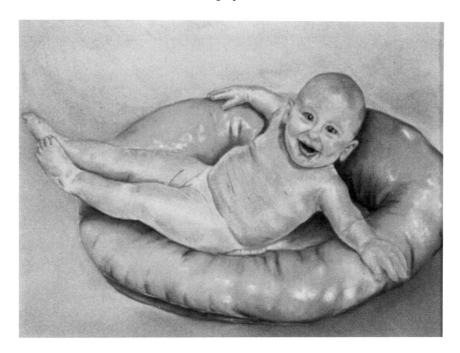

Figure 7. *Individuation, if you Please.* Oil on canvas, 24 x 36 inches.

Figure 8. *My Sleeping Beauties.* Oil on canvas, 18 x 24 inches.

Let me repeat that the fiction story is *inexactly* based on my memories growing up with my manic-depressive mother. Some of the writing was "souped up" but a lot of the story is true. When I finished Figure 6 and shared the work and the "pea story" with my therapist, Dr. Mitzner, I inquired about the accuracy of my memory. I had read this portion of my novel to a trusted friend, who attacked my accuracy of the scene with the butter knife. He stated matter-of-factly that there would have been oozing blood when Maida stabbed David. But my therapist, a medical doctor, informed me that my memory was indeed correct: puncture wounds do *not* bleed profusely until the instrument is removed. Her affirmation was reassuring and disturbing all at the same time: my memories were flooding back.

It is astounding what the dance of creativity can unfold. Yet, it makes inordinate sense. Many have researched this but probably none more ardently than Mihaly Csikszentmihalyi. In his latest text, *The Evolving Self,* he describes his research into creativity. Csikszentmihalyi (1993) spent copious hours studying artists in the act of painting. Just as I have described, he noted " . . . an almost hypnotic trance seemed to seize them as they struggled to give shape to their vision . . . they could not tear themselves away from it; they forgot hunger, social obligation, time and fatigue . . . But this fascination lasted only as long as a picture remained unfinished" (p. Xii). What Csikszentmihalyi discovered mirrors what every art therapist already knows and what Edith Kramer (1975) touted as sacrosanct in her heralded work *Art as Therapy with Children*: it is not the product but the ***process*** that matters.

Even in the first painting, Figure 5, the gateways were opening to my novel by way of the art process. Growing up, I recalled how much my mother adored fresh flowers. While she rarely received them, her artificial waxy and silk substitutes were a constant reminder of her desire. Moreover, flower motifs could be found everywhere. And when I looked to the fabric I had chosen for the still life (which required endless searching until I found the "perfect fabric"), I was again awestruck by the mere transference of taste. The tea cups, beautiful and devoid of sustenance are really quite obvious. As beautiful as they are, they begged to be filled with liquid, but instead, remain empty, void of liquid nurturance—how very fitting. While by now I was a mother myself, my perpetual search for a role model/mother was as endless as the cup rim itself.

Figure 6 has a multitude of meanings for me from the gold embroidery and pearls carefully sewn into the canvas to the actual act of *knifing* the linen in order to position the fork in place.

Metaphor can be really revealing in life. I have had a habit of nicknaming the people whom I hold dearest to my heart, "sweet pea." The original intent of this picture was quite joyous and connected to that vision. But often our psyches hold a different plan, one that is, in fact, more revealing, albeit, closer to the truth. While I religiously painted those peas into an almost sur-real reality, their life took on a meaning quite different from its original intent. When I created the painting, I worked it simultaneously with the rewriting of the aforementioned story. As a result, both works (the visual and the literal ones) influenced each other in ways that I would have neither pre-dicted nor foreseen. The way the two rubbed off on each other like twins of the same cell, yet wholly colored in a more fraternal fashion, astounded even me. My biography was in fact writing the biology (if you will) of my life's work. For, in fact, our work reflects our make-up, both from a biological and biographical viewpoint. Myss (1996) was quite literally on target when she pronounced this first principle of operation.

Just when I thought I was near completion of the painting (Figure 6), I pierced the canvas with a fork. The reason for using the fork was related to *my* part in my mother's collapse. If you remember, in the story, it was *I* that first catapulted that pea across the table into my brother's unsuspecting lap. I started the pea war and felt somewhat responsible for starting that whole sordid experience that led to my mother's eventual breakdown. What had originally been intended as a celebratory painting turned into a work of a dif-ferent color. Clearly, one that operated out of my darker side. Thus, the title, *The Lighter Side of Manic Depression* makes the work all the more ironic.

The next piece created, Figure 7 (see color insert), is related to Figure 6 but from a different developmental time. In becoming a mother, I struggled with my own unresolved childhood issues as well as the rearing of another human being. Sometimes to this day, I have felt unfit for such an arduous task. The reasons were many but most of them sprung from emptiness and lack of a role model. I felt terribly unsuited for such a task for a variety of reasons but the main conflict revolved around mothering. Having had a con-fused and unstable upbringing, truly I have struggled with the job of rearing children. Initially, this conflict caused me to reenter therapy with Dr. Mitzner as I desperately tried to resolve the endless conflict around my own separa-tion/individuation from that of my daughter's. Finding time for oneself when raising small children can be impossible at best. While many have written about this subject (specifically Edelman, 1994), it is still little comfort to be in the throes of such dichotomy. Mothering oneself is hard enough but con-tending with the demands of child rearing can be depressing, draining, and demanding as indicated in the abundant literature on the well-known state of postpartum depression. While I did not experience postpartum depression with either of my births, I certainly struggled with the demands of breast-feeding, working, and trying to be "all-parent." This struggle led me to inves-tigate these feelings not only through my artwork but also in discourse with my therapist, Dr. Mitzner.

In this painting, aptly titled "Individuation, if you please," my infant daughter, Kaitlyn, floats in her Tubby[c], and instead of basking in water, her bathtub floats in a heavenly sky. Thus the buoyancy is uplifted, if you will, to a different dimension. Unconsciously, I was attempting to make that leap, which is correlating individuation to a more ascendant plane on the developmental chain. The beginning of individuation also signaled an end of a developmental phase for Kaitlyn and me as her provider. I was very conscious of the developmental phases (from symbiosis to the rapprochement phase) going on in Kaitlyn but at the time, I was less developed in how this was influencing my personage and my perspective as a mother and also an artist/therapist. My daughter's individuation and separation from me was not a right of passage with which I struggled. In fact, I welcomed this developmental shift. But I felt enormously guilty. You see unlike other mothers that cried when their children took that first bus to kindergarten, I cheered. Before Kaitlyn was even born, I actually dreamt that she entered in a business suit, complete with 100 percent pinpoint Oxford dress shirt, tie, and carrying a briefcase. Talk about individuation, my psyche pushed Kaitlyn right past toilet training into the work force. It is not surprising that I struggled with such feelings, especially when surrounded by other mothers that cultivated such moments. While I enjoyed breastfeeding and this magical time with my children, I was simultaneously conflicted: I longed to return to the studio and separate from the constant demands of motherhood, a formidable task for which I felt ill-suited.

My life has been transformed and continues to be transposed by the people, events, readings and experiences in my life. As Myss (1996) aptly points out, this biography of events is what constitutes our biology and life purpose. And often times, our life's purpose is revealed in myriad ways.

In this next painting, the developmental struggle continued with the rearing of my children and myself. In Figure 8 (see color insert), my newborn son, Bryan, and three-year-old Kaitlyn are pictured dreaming together. Surrounding their pillow and blanket from top left to bottom right are: The Blessed Mother and the infant, Jesus; one of the seven dwarfs; Peter Pan; Snow White; the Baby from the now defunct television series Dinosaurs, and Wendy. The cartoon characters were selected because of their significance and influence on each of my children at this time in their lives. But the Blessed Mother and infant Jesus were a surprise, which I realized were created for me. At the very last moment when I thought I had finished the painting, I wiped out the makings of one more cartoon character and instead substituted the Holy Mother, Mary, and Jesus. Originally, I wasn't sure why I did this but perhaps my need for control was relinquished to this angelic duo to "watch over" and protect my children in ways that I could not, especially given my ongoing struggling with mothering and finding time for my own individuation. Conceivably the inclusion of the Blessed Mother and infant

Jesus had to do with my profound respect for miracles. For I am quite taken by the Saints and their teachings. As a *Course in Miracles* (1992) says: "Miracles are natural. Something is wrong when they don't happen." This was just the beginning of channeling myself towards a different axis and rotating from a different plane of existence. My relinquishing the care of my children to the Blessed Mother on an unconscious level made great sense since I felt unfit for the task. Naturally, the choice of someone so holy and unblemished as Mary made great sense. After all, the Madonna has been and continues to be the icon for the perfect mother, thus my attraction to the image and for all that it stands.

I have often referred to my mother-in-law, Carol Darby, as a saint. She has been a formidable influence in my life and that of my children. Like me, she resonates with the Blessed Mother and so when recently visiting her home and discussing this chapter, my eyes lighted on a painting that I had made as a gift for her for Easter (Figure 9), a copy from Rafael's works.

As I was telling her about this chapter and glanced at the painting above her head, I experienced "aesthetic arrest." I realized at that moment that Carol had been a substitute mother for me and that my attraction to the Madonna was one in the same, that is that ever-present struggle to find the perfect mother. In the previous painting, I relied on the Blessed Mother to

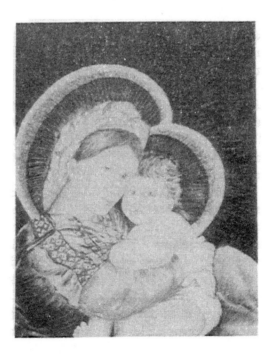

Figure 9. *Rafael's Mother and Child.*

take over and watch my children in ways that I could not and in the Rafael copy that I had given to my mother-in-law, I had transferred those feelings even more fully. Finally, I understood the need to transfer this weight to a higher plane.

Dreams are forebearers of our time. We can learn from them or ignore them. I tend to turn my rather deaf ear towards them as I search their herald for meaning in my life. Some of my clearest work and direction has come to me in dreams including the last book that I wrote (Horovitz-Darby, 1994). Dreams, are in fact, different levels of consciousness. Joseph Campbell, in *The Mythic Image*, details the seven power centers or Chakras of the Kundalini System. The sixth chakra named "Ajna" which means "Command" or the "Qualified Absolute" is located on the brow, dead center above the eyes. This positioning bespeaks a third eye, an inner eye and its job is "lessons related to mind, intuition, insight, and wisdom." Myss (1996) teaches "symbolic sight, the ability to use your intuition to interpret the power symbols in your life" (p. 57). Interpretation, however, is an outgrowth of reception. She stipulates quite directly that in order to receive information, one has to be clear and above all, "objective." Achterberg (1985) also discusses the concept of OOB (out of body) or "lucid dreaming" as to be coupled with "vivid imagery, a sense of dissociation" as well as akin to "shamanic seeing" (p. 28). Tart (1989) discussed "lucid dreaming" as a "growth experience." He states that the " . . . dreamer recognizes the intimate relation of his dream reality to his self; instead of fleeing from the Guardian . . . he looked him in the eye and embraced him, restoring the wholeness in his mind" (p. 21).

Recently, in pursuing the ways of Ai Gvdhi Waya as outlined in her book on shamanistic journeying through the concept of soul extraction and recovery, I started the first course in shamanistic journeys with one of her disciples, Odala Tlv DaTsi. Shortly after my first journey, I recorded some interesting dreams and discussed them with my Shaman, Odala Tlv DaTsi. His interpretation of one of my dreams led to a recent drawing in a workshop conducted by Bruce Moon, Ph.D., A.T.R. at the 28th annual American Art Therapy Association. We were instructed to draw any dream that we had (recurrent or otherwise) and then write a script for it. In doing so, it concretized the path that I am now on and in fact altered the title of this book.

After completing the drawing, we were instructed to write the text and go through a process with a dream guide (who mirrored back the exact reading of the script and continued to do so each time it was whittled down until it was only a sentence).

Here is the script written on the right side of the image:

I was standing at the edge of a large inviting hill, lush with green rolling grass and dirt brown sodden clay. As I approached the crevice and looked

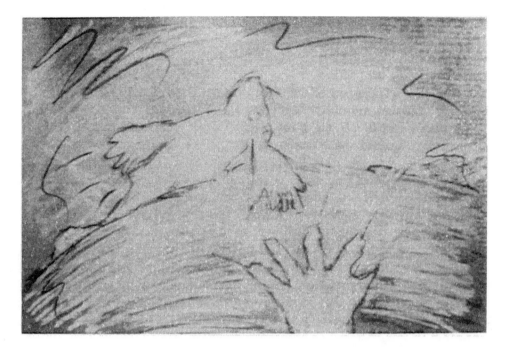

Figure 10. *A Leap of Faith.* Oil Craypas, 12 in. x 36 in.

down, I noticed the very steep quality of the decline: a cliff, which seemed to drop into the abyss forever.

Just then two children approached the precipice, gleefully stepped to the edge and their daring, darting eyes told next what they aimed to do.

Repeatedly, first one leapt off laughing enjoying the fall and then the other. As I desperately tried to reach out and stop the last one, the child just laughed and screamed, "No, don't stop me. I **want** to."

It was only then that I realized that this was not a desperate act but a **leap of faith.**

This process of the dream guide mirroring back the exact words scripted by the dreamer is a powerful, medicinal uptake in itself. But the process of honing down the contents of the script to a final sentence (each time repeated verbatim by the dream guide) an equally startling discovery can be made. In my final sentence, I wrote: "A child leapt off a cliff as I tried to stop him, but I realized that this was not a desperate act, but a leap of faith."

Yes, this was a leap of faith. Many of the players in dreams are just different aspects of our selves. In writing these powerful words, I realized that it was I that jumped repeatedly off that cliff and not with abandonment of purpose. No, on the contrary, the leap had great aim: that is one that would allow me to unfold continually to the process. As I have tried to evolve into a fuller human being, I have rediscovered how incredibly simple the method is for getting there. It is flow, continuous process, and elemental play. But staying in this creative state: well, there lies the rub.

And with patients, separation and dissociation from the person's issue while simultaneously remaining empathic enough to capture the essence of the person's suffering and guide him or her towards expression of that pain through the art is paramount in aiding the patient towards that final trajectory, self-propelled health.

To illustrate the importance of this, I will recount a story told to Myss (1996) during her earlier training in journalism. Her journalism professor spent a large amount of time emphasizing objectivity in reporting. The parable is quite interesting: She asked each of us to imagine that a building was on fire and that four reporters, each standing on a different corner, were covering the story. Each reporter would have a different view of the same event. Each would interview people on his or her corner. The question the teacher posed to us was: Which reporter had the real facts and accurate viewpoint?" And she then goes on to say, "Perhaps truth and reality are actually only matters of perception (p. 14)."

Myss (1996) stipulated that from that assignment she learned that: . . . detachment is essential to accomplishing an accurate evaluation. Nothing causes more interference than the need to be "right" or to prove that you can do an intuitive evaluation (p. 22).

Yes, the need to be "right" can be a daunting experience. About 16 years ago, I did a workshop for preschool teachers and as part of the instruction, I asked them to have their students do a drawing of themselves and their family doing something. (This is the simple instruction used by [Burns and Kaufman] (1972) in their now-heralded classic, *Action Styles and Symbols in Kinetic Family Drawings KFD*.) Without any more knowledge than the child's name, sex, and age, I was able to provide an accurate picture of their psychosocial histories as well as problem areas or strengths in school relations. Naturally, the teachers were amazed at my soothsayer-like ability. But as I pointed out to them, it was based on years of training as well as impartial objectivity and information I received from the picture itself. Above all, it didn't matter if my analysis were right or wrong. While I no longer like to partake in this analytic parlay, it is helpful to be able to transliterate and articulate such findings to other professionals. This process breeds greater understanding between the individual players that make up the treatment team of an individual. I simply presented what was being supplied to me.

It is really just a matter of fine-tuning my own frequency. But in order to do this on a continual basis, it is indeed necessary to be able to read the energy behind such matter.

Quantum physicists have confirmed the reality of the basic vibratory essence of life, clocking human DNA at a rate of 52 to 78 gigahertzes (billions of cycles per second). Although scientific instruments have not yet been able to determine one person's specific frequency and/or blocks to that energy, two basic facts have been determined: life energy is not static and that energy can be evaluated.

McNiff (1995) in his work *Earth Angels* talks about the property of matter and the energy relinquished to it and released by it. Our art and the artifacts of one's culture may be static energy but they are enlivened and in fact animated by the energy bestowed by their makers. Perhaps this could be called the "God Principle." If humankind is "made in the image of God," then don't we do the same: that is, make things with our imagery in mind and therefore leave an indelible print on society?

What caused me to really think about this was a remarkable article that appeared in the *Science Times* section of the *New York Times* on September 21, 1996 entitled "Archaeologists in Australia Find Earliest Signs of Artistic Behavior." This discovery predated the cave paintings by 15,000 years. This stunning discovery predated people's occupation of Australia from 116,000 years ago to as much as 176,000 years ago. Naturally, this has had a reverberating influence on the origins of human creativity since scholars have "long identified cave and rock art as a defining characteristic of modern Homo sapiens."

Of unique interest were the carvings themselves. On one small area of rock, the scientists counted 3,500 circles. On still another rock, just a few feet away, 3,200 more circles had been etched. The archaeologists calculated that each circle would take at least an hour to complete: "If one person worked for eight hours each day, the entire display would have taken nearly 900 days to complete. In a society where every day must have been a struggle for survival . . . the task must have been one of enormous cultural importance" (Nobel, 1996).

Or perhaps this was not the mark of Homo sapiens at all. Fred Smith, a paleontologist at Northern Illinois University in DeKalb stated in this article: "We make assumptions that art has to relate to humans, but there's no reason for that thinking. One shouldn't jump to conclusions that if there's art at that age, then that means we have to be dealing with what is thought of as modern humans" (Noble, 1996).

After reading this article, I immediately exclaimed that this need to create is why we do what we do. This is the raison d'être for Art Therapy: it is the ultimate search for meaning in the culture of humankind, it is the study in understanding our first language, the primal pump. Naturally, some of my students probably thought I had gone over the edge. In the words of Carl Sagan who authored this idea in his last movie and book *Contact*, the constant search for life's purpose is in fact "a journey to the heart of the Universe."

There are many ways to travel and just as many cultures espousing ways in which to inventory the riches of our lives. Journeying to that center varies from meditative stances of Buddhism to delegated prayer. How one gets there is matter of choice and inner guidance. There are many ways that I find center. But one method is through the vehicle of art. As I stated in the Introduction: art transcends all time, all space, and all language. In essence, I become an instrument for the art. Instead of it becoming the vehicle for me, in reality, I am the conduit for its influence. Often times, while in this state of *elemental play*, I feel akin to a person at an Ouija® board. The "imageorator" that Moon (1996) speaks about is really what is at work during these times. The propensity for communication is at an all time high during this stage.

My sister-in-law, Valerie Saalbach, an opera singer, described this centering as it came to her in dream form. In the dream, she saw herself as a "single musical note cascading with a greater instrument," the symphony of humankind, if you will (Saalbach, 1997). Her dream informed something in me. That is how we view ourselves according to our plane of communication.

Being more visually-oriented, I have always looked at things from the perspective of being a spoke on the cogwheel. Is it no wonder that I view myself in a more constructed way than my musically-oriented sister-in-law, who perceives herself in a more aural manner? Perhaps that is why I began making clay drums a few years ago. This incessant need to communicate, like described in the findings of the previous cited 1996 article in the *New York Times*, may in fact be a greater part of my archetypal unconscious than I am

Figure 11. *Psycho-acoustics or She Hit the Nail Right on the Head.* Clay drum, 20 in. x 24 in. x 20 in.

able to understand. The pictures of my next three works bespeak my need to "communicate" in a more aural and literal way.

This drum and its title was an intentional play on words and art (e.g., "she hit the nail right on the head" has more than the mere meaning of the nails decorating the drum head of the skin). Drumming, by definition, is a pounding communication. The hammer, visually piercing the walls of the clay, is meant to imply the manner in which humankind breaks the sound waves of our culture. I loved making this drum. It required over 50 hours of painting and blowtorching the walls with an oxyacetylene torch in order to acquire the bronzed patina on the elbow, fist, and body parts that protrude from various openings around the drum wall. My need to make an instrument is related to my love of musical instruments (I play guitar and drums, of course) but more importantly, the act of making a drum was intentionally connected to my deep-seated desire to communicate with and to others. In times past and present, Indians have used drums to beat out their messages. In our now less primitive times, we have all kinds of ways in which to transmit our thoughts to others. But somehow, the ancient ways bespeak a power that we seem to have lost. My drum making is an attempt to reconnect with that on a very sacred level. Thus my work can be realistically tailored or playfully humorous as in this next drum:

Again, the title is invested in literal and aural concerns since Beowulf is connected to both principles articulated in the aforementioned paragraph.

Figure 12. *Beowulf Speaks.* Clay drum, 18 in. x 15 in. x 10 in.

The comical wolf leaping out of the clay walls again bespeaks my need for connection to others, even in the form of animal spirits. What I see now as comically unconscious is my decision to detail the glazed body of the wolf in a "checkered" pattern. Considering how often I have referred to my memories being "checkered by my mother's nervous breakdowns" of all the ways in the world to glaze this wolf, it is quite revealing that I spent the time painstakingly articulating the checkered pattern.

In this next drum, I am not certain of its meaning or the reasoning behind having hands at north, south, east, and west directions, but I can guess at the compass of its significance. Atop of the drum skin are unisex humans dancing in somewhat tribal fashion. This particular drum was perhaps the most influential since it was personally created to mimic my own hand and so in many respects it is in and of my hand. But its need to act as a kind of direction-finder is intriguing. Perhaps it was meant as an inner guide for my own centering and inner journey. I do know that when I play the drum either in conjunction with others or alone, that I feel very much as if I have found my way and perhaps, too, my voice.

As I have stated before, my creative urges spring from a variety of sources. Whether they are penned through poetic endeavors, novels, non-fiction, or

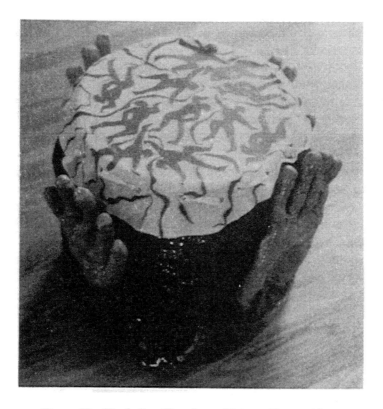

Figure 13. *Hands On.* Clay drum, 20 in. x 18 in. x 15 in.

made from artistic media, it all seems connected to the same purpose: expression of creativity. Without that expressive output, I am in a constipated state. Like the bodily functions that control the release of our waste system, I, too, find myself needing to purge myself of these creative urgings on as regular a basis as possible. At the 28th American Art Therapy Association conference, Don Jones, H.L.M., A.T.R., suggested the commitment of practicing art for a minimum of one hour per day. This is an excellent suggestion to make art therapists the practice of what it is we preach.

For me, going to an art therapy conference where I actively commune with other art therapists can be a bit more like church and community than going to a house of worship. The energy that I tap into at those conferences is indeed sacred. At a recent art therapy conference, I had the unique experience of writing with Lynn Kapitan, A.T.R., B.C., for the opening ceremonies of the 29th annual American Art Therapy Association conference. The result led to Chapter 5, the dragon lore story. Had I not written back and forth with Lynn via file exchanges through e-mail, I probably would not have written the story or the chapter. Writing with another human being has been an unparalleled experience, much akin to dancing. I had to learn to follow the rhythm of another and simultaneously create my own way. In this case, the writing process informed the artistic process and vice versa since a performance piece resulted from this exchange. If I were to try and decipher an exact rhythm, it would be similar to the old proverb, "Which came first, the chicken or the egg?"

While there seems to be no answer to that question, equally as baffling to me is how that creative process gets separated out. In fact, for me, it doesn't. Instead, it remains enmeshed, happily processed, connecting from one creative synapse to the next until some sense of completion is felt. While many artists plunge into the doldrums of depression when completing a creative work, I am often in the stage of my next work even before I have finished the last project. However, accomplishing and finalizing a task has been maddening for many, including authors like Virginia Woolf: "Like many artists, however, every time she finished an important work she went into mourning, feeling as empty and bereft as if she had suffer the death of a loved one" (Bond, 1989, p. 101).

I am certain that when feelings like the aforementioned arise that creative artists become blocked. For some, this is temporary. For others, it can be crippling, much like a dis-ease. Moreover, I believe that ennui is a major component of such blockage. Just as fat accumulates in the arteries and clogs the heart's ventricles, boredom clouds the spirit, and cuts off creative potential. While there are many steps that one can take to "fix" such a problem, I truly believe that centering one's core is at the root of such ministry. How one attains that centering is as individually tailored as DNA and for some it may take on the work espoused in Waya's treatise, *Soul, Recovery and Extraction*. Through shamanism, a technique as old as humankind, an individual is moved into an altered state and travels the inner dimensions of what is referred to as nonphysical reality. The process of journeying with a shaman for the purpose of soul recovery is about: ". . . regaining the fragments of one's soul energy that has been trapped, lost or stolen either by another person or through a traumatic incident that has occurred in one's life" (Waya, 1992, p. i). The process is done via Extraction where the tool within the shamanistic tradition: ". . . dissolves blocks from our bodies or the aura of electromagnetic energy that surrounds us" (Waya, 1992, p. i).

Then there are others such as Cameron (1992) who offer exercises to unleash the creative spirit and help the artist remain block-free. While there are many ways to unlock the creative agent, the pathway to excavating that potential is always available, although for some it lies dormant. The extraction lies in releasing the agent into an atmosphere of continual flow and then the process becomes self-generative. Of interest, is the similarity that I have read repeatedly in various research from Myss' *Anatomy of the Spirit*, which is about her career as a medical intuit and utilizing the principles that are based in Chakras, Sacraments and the Seifrot (Kabbalah), to the practice of Waya's *Soul Recovery and Extraction* as described in the methodology of shamanism and altered states. It matters little how one travels in order to clean up the baggage of the tattered portions of one's soul; more important is the desire to change and get to that place of harmony, inner peace, soul-making, *elemental play*, and *soulution*. But, discovering its existence doesn't affirm its placement: practice does.

Practice makes perfect. This drawing is from an old photograph taken by my father of my siblings and me. Sitting left to right, I am pictured age 6, my sister, Nancy, age 10, and my brother is age 8. In the background, is the family piano, handed down from one generation to the next. This Baldwin™, originally played by my father's mother, Dena, was the piano that started my brother's astounding musical career.

My family photographs have always held very personal meaning for me. As a child, I would pore over these snapshots that forever captured time in my life, my family, and the family that went before me. My children do the same thing. Often, I find Kaitlyn or Bryan rifling through family albums sometimes retrieving a personal memory. Whenever I would return home from being away for a long period of time, the first thing that I would do (and that my siblings also did) would be to open the dining room drawer where my mother had thrown hundreds of snapshots and family albums. Going through these visual times past was a comfort to me and to my siblings. It was akin to an old "blankie" that comforted me through the ages. As a result, many of my paintings and drawings stem from capturing those moments. This drawing is one of those attempts.

Figure 14. *The Talents.* Pencil Drawing, 9 in. x 12 in.

The title "The Talents" merely explains our similarity. All three of us are chock full of talent, varied and plentiful. Of that I am eternally grateful. While I used to view my talent as somewhat of a curse (having so much energy can often dampen the spirits of others), I have finally come to accept its place in my life. Of interest is the fact that I purposely detailed the upper half of the photograph while simultaneously choosing not to finish off the lower half of the picture.

According to the "undeveloped" areas, the lower undefined areas would be the Chakras Muladhara (Chakra 1)(Root System), Svadisthana (Chakra 2)(Her Special Abode) and the Manipura (Chakra 3)(City of the Shining Jewel). In terms of power centers, Myss (1996) states these stand for (a) Tribal Power (Chakra 1), that is all that you receive from your archetypal and communal family, (b) Relationship Power (Chakra 2), relationships that shift from obeying tribal authority to discovering other relationships which satisfy personal, physical needs (usually starting at around age 7), and (c) Personal Power (Chakra 3), containing the issues related to the development of personal power and self-esteem. In looking at this, I instead detailed the upper Chakras, which have more to do with the nurturant system and that of the intellectual properties. Interestingly enough, I was seven in this picture. Perhaps, too, my leaving the bottom three Chakras unfinished speaks to my need to redo my family of origin issues (Tribal Power) as well as the areas of personal power and self-esteem (Relationship and Personal Power Issues). Burns and Kaufman (1972) as well as Hammer (1975) would concur with Myss' interpretations since lack of detail in the bottom portion of the person would suggest the same. Both the art and conceptual system described seem to quite aptly articulate my struggle. Considering what I had been unmasking in personal therapy, that came as little surprise.

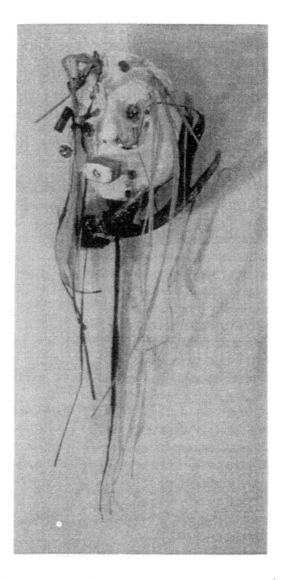

Figure 15. *No More Secrets*. Mixed media-plaster gauze, sterling silver wire, African beads, deer antlers, broken lock, and raffia.

Speaking of unmasking, "No More Secrets" was cast from my face and then augmented with the various attached artifacts. It is difficult, at best, for me to write about this piece since the decoration had both personal and sacred meaning. It started on a Sunday walk in my backwoods. Alone in the serenity of my most hallowed and treasured woods, I walked along the creek adjacent to my wooded property. There before me were these antlers hanging in a tree. It was unclear whether or not they had been cast off by a deer or cut off by a hunter. I climbed up the tree, took these wondrous frontal spikes, and sat down by the creek to study their bony surface. As I pondered their beauty, I placed one under my chin and the other alongside my face, much like that which is pictured in the final product. It reminded me of the thinker in animal form.

Late that night, I glanced at the antlers lying beside my unfinished mask and felt the urge to work on it. As I wired the antlers to the mask, the beaded elements fell into place. The broken lock was added last. Intrinsically, I knew the lock's meaning was tied into my acceptance of my-then broken marriage and the fragmented portion of my soul. When I completed it, however, I felt stronger inside as if a great weight had been released and let go. As well, I was able to really begin the process of talking about these feelings in my therapy with Dr. Mitzner. The name had to do as much with the work in therapy as well as the shame that I had harbored around my failed relationship. While the marriage ending was neither my initiation nor my fault, I have accepted my share in its demise. As most know, there are many versions to a story. In this case, there was my story, his story, and then the real story, which lies somewhere in between. Finally, I gave myself permission to move on from this very painful place and accepted this new face, which I finally adopted as a result of the marital separation.

What became clear to me through this last work was how very invested I am in the creative process. I often stated that if I could couple with my work, that I would be forever content. The reasons are myriad but primarily it has to do with consistency, nurturance, and dependability. I have always been able to count on my art, my work, and myself. In fact, it has and continues to be the most consistent relationship that I have ever sustained. It is always there for me. It doesn't talk back (although it certainly dialogues with me) and it is something on which I can always depend. My artistic functioning, this consolation of my somewhat tattered soul has served me well. And it never leaves me or lets me down. This self-perpetuating affliction which drives me to the brink of my shadow and then back renders me well. It is a curse and a gift. It is neither either/or, it is both/and.

I have come a long way through my work. It has been and continues to be a lifelong process. While reviewing it "objectively" (if that were even possible) is really not plausible since I am the maker, my subjective inquiry has been an intriguing journey. In becoming more aware of my inner language system, I become healthier and more whole. As Myss (1996) states: "Learning the language of the human energy system is a means to self-understanding . . . by gaining fluent knowledge of energy anatomy . . . you will be able to read your own body like a scripture" (p. 7). Myss went on to say that it is "work" to discover ourselves and that identity is based on self discovery, not biologic or ethnic inheritance. In other words, this rabble-rouser stuff of the first order is in and of itself a revolution. As I work toward that end, I intertwine that dance with my work and essentially it becomes woven into the strands of artistic therapy. It is that which I aim to do.

The Soul selects her own Society
Then—shuts the Door
To her divine Majority
Present no more

Unmoved—she notes the Chariots—pausing
At her low Gate
Unmoved—an emperor be kneeling
Upon her Mat

I've known her—from an ample nation
Choose One
Then—close the Valves of her attention
Like Stone.

EMILY DICKINSON, 1890

Chapter 2

THE DISSOCIATED SELF OR TRUE INDIVIDUATION

According to the DSM IV-R (the highly revered manual of psychiatric disorders), there is a disease called "Depersonalization Disorder (300.6)." In this manual, its distinguishing hallmarks are characterized as follows:

A. Persistent or recurrent experiences of feeling detached from, and as if one is an outside observer of, one's mental processes or body (e.g., feeling like one is in a dream).

B. During the depersonalization experience, reality testing remains intact.

C. The depersonalization causes clinically significant distress or impairment in social, occupational, or other important areas of functioning.

D. The depersonalization experience does not occur exclusively during the course of another mental disorder, such as Schizophrenia, Panic Disorder, Acute Stress Disorder, or another Dissociative Disorder, and is not due to the direct psychological effects of a substance (e.g., a drug of abuse, medication) or a general medical condition (e.g., temporal lobe epilepsy).

American Psychiatric Association, 1994, p. 490

I call the reader's attention to these descriptions for a variety of reasons but mostly because the inherent nature of slipping into a state of "depersonalization" is akin to what happens in the creative state. The first definition, "persistent or recurrent experiences of feeling detached from, and as if one is an outside observer of, one's mental processes or body (e.g., feeling like one is in a dream)" reminds me well of what it feels like when in the trance-like state of creating a work of art.

In a personal communication with poet Elizabeth Salomea Gray (1998), she wrote:

Through image, the more common language than words, that deep unconscious primal place, we as human beings return to the differentiated state where we are working with essence to create healing; during the process of realizing that image and embodying it in the creation of art, we redifferentiate who we are as self, coming up different, healed, more integrated, recreated.

Elizabeth Salomea Gray's description of that creative state embodies the reintegration of self in a way that reminds me of what occurs in cells that regenerate, as cited in the previous works of Ford (1992) and Becker (1985). In fact, this definition of differentiation sets the stage for the healing process and contributes to the direction towards a more holistic self.

While I could sculpt from memory by the time I was five and copy anything by the age of eight, I remember how awe-struck I was when I learned the color theory of the impressionists and studied Johannes Itten's *The Art of Color*. When I awakened to seeing color values and negative and positive space, the way in which I perceived the world completely changed. And when I drafted something in front of me, I dissociated or as Gray put it "recreated." This was practically taught by all of my master teachers as they urged me to distance enough from the subject in order to decipher it, reproduce it, and empathically capture its essence. And when working with patients, is it really all that different? It is a delicate balance between separation and dissociation from the patient's issue while simultaneously remaining empathic enough to capture the essence of the person's suffering and guide him or her toward expression of that pain through the art.

Moon referred to this altered state as "creative immersion." In one of the more important thrusts of his opus, Moon's concept of "creative immersion" assembled the state in which the artist/writer/dancer/musician/creative spirit becomes absorbed in the creative process and remains little more than the messenger to the medium. It was with great aplomb that he described this position: "At the height of my creative work it sometimes seems as if there is an image-orator and I am little more than a stenographer. In these times, I have lost contact with the world around me and become immersed in an imaginal inner existence . . . this encounter may best be described as creative immersion" (Moon, 1996, p. 125).

In Search of Self: Informing the Process

So perhaps the real question is whether or not in the state of "creative immersion" the artist is truly depersonalized (as defined by the DSM IV) or merely in what I would term a healthy dissociative state. Truly, what I am suggesting is that individuation is a by-product of this dissociative condition.

According to some existentialist theories (such as that of Sartre), when one looks deeply inside the self, before birth or forward beyond death, he/she finds a void. Nothing. If capable of tossing aside all memory, knowledge and sensation, the vista holds the core center as an ego, formless and inconceivable like the nucleus of an electron. By focusing attention on this nothing within the self, the concept is gradually transformed into the abstraction of nothingness. Nothingness, one of the truly great accomplishments of human sensibility, is a force, a ground, in a certain sense *the* reality. From this axis comes humankind's despair, but also, if he or she has courage, existential integrity. While Dostoevski wrote, "Suffering is the origin of consciousness," Sartre wrote with equal lucidity, "Life begins on the other side of despair."

For me, Sartre is the quintessential existentialist fiction writer who operates from a Cartesian tradition. At the inception of any investigation, he examines the *cognito*, the self-that-is and the self that observes the self-that-is. From this dualistic positioning, he moves endlessly through brilliant progressions of: knowing-doing, being-becoming, nature-freedom, et cetera. And only through the self does he allow the drama of truth to unfold.

It is that exact locale that is operational for the artist truly immersed in the state of creativity. Researchers have described this "creative immersion" in varied manner. For example, Hammer (1990) elevated the art of traditional verbal psychotherapy to a science akin to verbal Jin Shin Jyutsu. With extraordinary skill and candor, he was able to break through the most hardened patient veneers by utilizing imagery that "bubbled up" when he was entrenched in this creative state. In one vignette, he recounted the story of a floridly psychotic patient engaged in non-stop chatter while pacing throughout their session. All he had to do was merely wonder out loud as to what might happen if she arrested her discourse much the same way a soldier comes to a standstill when he is not "marching back and forth" but merely "at ease." His verbal and visual interpretation literally halted her right in her tracks. He likened this verbal interpretation to an art form that could in fact be developed, honed, and crafted much like a fine work of art. And in his book, filled with both humorous and poignant anecdotes, he offers the reader direction in developing this skill of creative immersion. Above all, he recommends paying attention to and honoring the role of "humor" in therapy.

Creativity seems to be inherently guided necessary perhaps for survival. Otherwise ennui, emptiness, and despair set in. Moon (1996) reiterates the position of faith and hope in the process of therapy. He emphasizes the importance of true art both in the therapeutic process as well as attending to the "prevalent disorder affecting . . . twentieth century (society) (that) . . . is existential emptiness"(p. 5). He sees this as "loss of soul" and refers to others (Moore, 1993, McNiff, 1993, Hillman, 1989) who have viewed this same ennui as a pathological predicament of our society. In case vignettes, Moon illustrates again and again that as the artist/patient experiences success in his/her ability to handle media and solve creative dilemmas, "the capacity to deal with other aspects of life is enhanced." He furthermore suggests that the "*quality* of our patient's artwork, and our own, be taken seriously." Furthermore, he implores promotion not only of ventilation of feelings but skillful and "articulate artistry" (Moon, 1996, p. 88).

Bergman, Witzum, and Bergman (1991) in discussing Shiatsu as a strategic tool in psychotherapy also highlighted the evocative power of the non-verbal therapies when traditional approaches (verbal) have failed: ". . . in cases where there is dissociation of affect from certain verbal content (as in Alexythemia), the client can derive no benefits from psychotherapy . . . in such cases a number of non-verbal techniques can be used to bring about a therapeutic breakthrough such as dance therapy, music therapy, and art therapy" (p. 9).

Many art therapists have concurred that cognitive and developmental gains go hand in hand with positive emotional and behavioral changes. (Henley, 1992; Horovitz-Darby, 1988, 1991, 1994; Kramer, 1975; Moon, 1990; Moon, 1996; Naumburg, 1980; and Silver, 1970, 1976,1989).

Likewise, there have been some that have positioned themselves fervently as conduits to therapy only as orators to the image. Moon (1996) forcefully determines that his efficacy in exacting health comes not from interpretation of the image but merely from facilitating its entranceway. By necessity, he suggests that art therapists become the channels for this through "artistic psychology." He contends that to interpret an image breeds "imagicide" that is "diagnosing an image into the position of disease and thus annihilating its importance to the maker via interpretation" (Horovitz, 1998).

While I certainly agree in theory, because art therapy currently seems to be embedded in a classical medical model, it is often necessary to be able to translate these images into medical context and jargon. While I certainly hope that all clinicians will soon understand the magic of engaging the soul in art making, I think it is advantageous to be schooled in interpretation in order to communicate with all health professionals regarding what it is that we do and what it is that images seem to be projecting of the patient. How we *do* therapy with the patient is an altogether different manner. How we *practice* this business of soul making is what truly is essential in the salubrious treatment of the heart, mind and spirit of the person and *that* is what this book is about.

Soul making. This is a lifelong process that constantly challenges the spirit into change and evolution. Life is never homogenous. Instead, the heterogeneous mixture often results in confusion, doubt, and sometimes illness. To aid the passage toward wellness and health, a certain degree of pathology is always present and perhaps even necessary. After all, wellness cannot be instated in an environment immune to disease. To put it more precisely, the trajectory towards wellness implies a certain degree of pathoformicity, or the darker side.

On Creativity, Self, and Psychosis

This creative state can paradoxically be both a gift and a curse. For example, the dip into creativity can reveal startling information to the psyche. And there are costs involved in this aim. For some, relationships may be sacrificed, causing great alarm and psychic undoing. It is a delicate balance, this creativity. While it can cause unparalleled surges in mood and heightened awareness in others, it may constrict and shrivel up one's resonance with reality, plummeting some into the doldrums of despair. One need only look to some of the greatest artists of our time for examples of this: (e.g., van Gogh, Hemingway, Schumann, etc.) In a chapter devoted entirely to manic-depressive illness, creativity and leadership, Goodwin and Jamison (1990, p. 347) table just a partial listing of major twentieth century American poets, born between 1895 and 1935, with documented histories of manic-depressive illness. These include Hart Crane (1899-1932), Theodore Roethke (1908-1963), Delmore Schwartz (1913-1966), John Berryman (1914-1972), Randall Jarrell (1914-1935), Robert Lowell (1917-1977), Anne Sexton (1928-1974), and Sylvia Plath (1932-1963). (Of course, there are also some that argue this case, suggesting that medical records were not well kept and thus compiling evidence posthumously would be a preposterous position. (See Gutin, 1996.)

According to Goodwin and Jamison (1990)," . . . among writers, poets appear the most likely to suffer from manic-depressive illness, many novelists, playwrights, and others have as well" (p. 347).

Virginia Woolf, probably the most celebrated manic-depressive writer of our time, described this toll that manic-depressive illness exacted on her life. In writing about these experiences, her peaks and her valleys (or antithetically) her climbs and her dives, she said: "How far do our feelings take their colour from the dive underground? I mean, what is the reality of any feeling?" (Goodwin & Jamison, 1992, p.18) Her husband, Leonard Woolf, (1964), likened the relationship of her illness to her literary creativity: "The creative imagination in her novels, her ability to 'leave the ground' in conversation, and the voluble delusions of the breakdowns all came from the same place in her mind—she 'stumbled after her own voice' and followed the voices that fly ahead" (p. 347).

In *An Unquiet Mind*, psychologist, Kay Jamison, wrote a stunning account of her manic-depressive bouts and the phases that propelled her into these altered states of creative immersion, and boundless productivity. But like everything, her mania and productivity resulted in enormous costs. In her worst manic bouts, she was wrestled to the ground, fitted in a four-point leather restraint, and finally institutionalized. Of these darker periods she wrote:

Well you are not like the rest of us, meaning among other things, to be reassuring. But I compare myself with my former self, not with others. Not only that, I tend to compare my current self with the best I have been, which is when I have been mildly manic. When I am present "normal" self, I am far removed from when I have been my liveliest, most productive, most intense, most outgoing and effervescent. In short, for myself, I am a hard act to follow. And I miss Saturn very much. (Jamison, 1995, p. 92)

While Jamison (1995) is caustic in her final remark, the "high" associated with those highly productive and creative outpourings are indeed difficult to surrender. She wrote:

> . . . however dreadful these moods and memories have been, they are always offset by the elation and vitality of others; and whenever a mild and gentlish wave of brilliant and bubbling manic enthusiasm comes over me, I am transported by its exuberance–as surely as one is transported by a pungent scent into a world of profound recollection–to earlier more intense and passionate times. Still the seductiveness of these unbridled and intense moods is powerful; and the ancient dialogue between reason and the senses is almost always more interestingly and passionately resolved in favor of the senses. (pp. 211-212)

In fact, she went on to discuss, how much she wrestled with relinquishing these more creative periods in her life:

> I found my milder manic states powerfully inebriating and very conducive to productivity. I couldn't give them up. More fundamentally, I genuinely believed–courtesy of strong-willed parents, my own stubbornness, and a WASP military upbringing–that I ought to handle whatever difficulties came my way without having to rely upon crutches such as medication. (p. 99)

Still at the same time, Jamison struggled with her dichotomized ways and longed for normalcy while maintaining the high from her creative state.

> I understand why Jekyll killed himself before Hyde had taken over completely. I took a massive dose of lithium with no regrets. ... Suicidal depression, I decided in the midst of my indescribably awful, eighteen month bout of it, is God's way of keeping manics in their place. It works. Profound melancholia is a day-in, day-out, night-in, night-out, almost arterial level of agony. It is a pitiless, unrelenting pain that affords no window of hope, no alternative to a grim and brackish existence, and no respite from the cold undercurrents of thought and feeling that dominate the horrible restless nights of despair. (p. 114)

Clearly, Jamison grappled with these altered states for a variety of reasons, some of which definitively included her struggle around relinquishing her incredible productivity level while immersed in the manic state. Yet, without these manic episodes, bursts of creativity and focused immersion, she admitted her productivity would have been greatly impaired. Luckily, Jamison was able to find the correct dose of lithium carbonate to both balance these episodic swings while tempering her creativity so that she could remain centered, productive, and above all, composed. However, many were not so lucky. Lithium carbonate was only discovered as a prophylactic for manic-depressive illness in 1969. Before that time, some of our greatest writers, musicians, and artists suffered from this insidious disease without pharmaceutical treatment.

Moreover, Goodwin and Jamison (1992) reported that novelists and poets suffered the most elated mood states, whereas the playwrights and artists were the most likely to report severe mood swings (p. 353). Again, there might be many (such as Gutin, 1996) who would question the sampling procedure of these artists as trustworthy. Goodwin and Jamison further indicated that oddly enough, many creative writers, artists and musicians suffered greatly from manic-depression yet renounced the use of psychopharmacological intervention. "Writers and artists frequently express concern about the effects of psychiatric treatment on their ability to create and produce; these concerns are especially pronounced when it comes to taking medication. This mistrust reflects unfounded preconceptions, fears of altering long-established work patterns and rituals, or simple resistance to treatment" (Goodwin & Jamison, 1992, p. 364).

So even now in the advent of ample psychotropic offerings, there are many creative souls that would prefer to walk that uncertain line of despair rather than relegate the high associated with "ritualistic" creativity to pharmaceutical intervention. As both a writer and artist, I can strongly relate to that position. While no one disputes that medication is the front-line treatment for manic-depressive patients and psychotherapy alone would be indefensible, it has been suggested that psychotherapy coupled with pharmacological treatment has an additive independent impact on the course of properly medicated manic-depressive illness. (Alas, this is only true for those that can tolerate the intensity of the psychotherapeutic relationship.) Jamison and Goodwin (1992) emphasized the importance of a trusting, honest, and empathic relationship in assuring good outcome in pharmacological treatment.

According to Kahn (1990), who discussed psychotherapy with manic patients, mania "turns the doctor-patient relationship upside down" (p. 230). Reasons for this vary, but among the chief reasons listed is that of vicarious empathic listening rooted in enticement, a reward in itself. According to Kahn, manic patients experience a true "silver lining" which is akin to the goals of psychotherapy. Those positive changes are "sensitivity, sensual intensity, productivity, creativity, social ease, and outgoingness" (p. 230). Some patients seem willing to "sell their soul" for the high of hypomania.

Having personally benefited from the high associated with productivity, hypomania and creativity, I can attest to its addictive qualities. When I am in the throes of creation, I become quite lost to all that surrounds me. I literally sit at my computer for almost a half day before biological urges (such as eating or waste elimination) cause me to take notice of other inner and outer realities. The same is true for my art. I can work at an easel or sculpt clay for hours on end and if outside demands didn't trigger a change from that vantage point, I would happily continue.

Of course, such artistic posture has had costs. While I have lived a rather prolific life and immersed myself in aesthetic activities as long as I can remember, there has been good reason for such enterprise. In part, my departure into artistic outlets was an abreaction to my own mother's manic-depressive illness. It became a self-soothing, almost maternal replacement for what I never received in mothering. In short, I "recreated" myself anew which bore both societal approval and personal success. Yet, the upshot has probably caused me to become addicted to this position. And while creating certainly nurtures me, it is incessantly demanding in its need for release. Naturally, this makes for a rather uneasy bedfellow. And thus, it has ended in personal costs and many hours spent in therapy attempting to wed my artistic license with everyday life. This has been and continues to be a life-long struggle.

Many have agreed (English, 1949) that schizophrenics are more easily treated since the manic-depressive patient rejects the analyst, unsure that he/she needs the therapeutic patient-doctor relationship at all. According to Fromm-Reichmann (1949), psychotherapy with manic-depressive patients fails due to their "unyielding grandiosity." As a result, the manic-depressive patient lacks close interpersonal relatedness and thus the cost described earlier in relationship-making.

Probably the most pointed opinion regarding psychotherapy's impact is that of Kahn (1990). He proposed that mania has been understood, as analytic theory has long contended, primarily as a "denial against depression," although it has been cleverly pointed out that depression could be the next morning's guilty defense against the regretted manic outbursts. What Kahn so clearly points out is that in aiding manic-depressive illness, the focus has tended to minister the depression, ignoring the mania. This well-taken point leaves the bulk of creative manic-depressives feeling overwhelmed by the loss of productivity, sedated if you will into societal platitudes, while clinicians steadfastly ignore their incessant compass toward sanity: creativity.

Personally, productivity is in fact closely connected with my sanity, it is in fact a high-ranking mechanism for my survival. Survival can be defined in ranges from providing sustenance, clothing, and protection, to the evolutionary mechanism. For me, while the necessities of life have real bearing in how responsibly I operate in this society, it is the quest towards creativity and understanding, and its impact on my personal platform that indeed stimulates growth in me as an organism. Lewin (1951) most poetically summed up the analytic view of mania's impetus towards creativity as an "elated return to endless satiety at the mother's breast."

Having grown up in a household controlled by my mother's manic depression outbursts, Lewin's statement gave me much pause as I looked to my own issues and a painting which I had included in my book, *Spiritual Art*

Therapy: An Alternate Path. While the topic of manic-depression was not forefront in my mind when I created the image in Figure 16, the concept of satiety was. But its stimulus aroused issues of satiety and abuse in the treatment of a suicidal patient who witnessed it in process in my studio/private practice office. The fact that the painting stimulated my patient's issues regarding satiety (and lack thereof) was an unexpected twist of events that allowed for greater introspection in her treatment.

Moreover, the need to capture my son's satiety, perhaps, on a deeper level, was the desire to capture my own lost youth: that is the sustenance that I had so craved and never received from my manic-depressive mother, constantly unattainable to provide such a reserve. Breastfeeding was always such an important connection between my children and me. Is it no wonder that

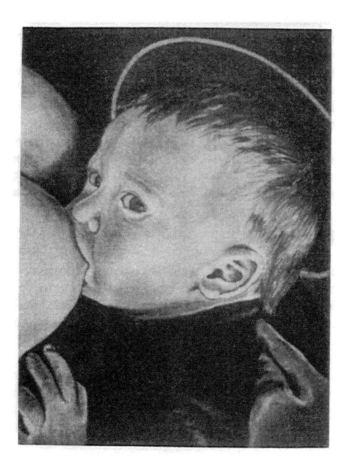

Figure 16. *Heaven Scent.* Oil on canvas and 24 karat gold leaf. 18 in. x 24 in.

I wanted to offer up my breast and offer then all that I had never received and (still) so desperately sought?

I can remember growing up and wondering why my mother never elected verbal psychotherapy for the treatment for her manic-depression. In time, it became abundantly clear that the thinking in the sixties and seventies was to sedate and medicate manic-depressive patients rather than dive into their psyches; the reason probably remains the same today: clinicians refer to it as "Band-Aid Therapy." Alas, no different today, this approach is in place due to managed care (and/or spiraling cost controls). Kahn (1990) reported that euphoric hypomania requires "complex decision making" since it holds the potential to be productive or destructive. As well, countertransference, envy, and identification (e.g., listening to vicarious accounts of artistic, financial, or sexual fantasies) can stimulate the therapist to keep the patient forever. Instead, an optimal countertransference might include "pleasurable appreciation of the omnipotential fantasies of the hypomanic, tempered by a savvy, watchful eye and a willingness to confront poor judgment" (p. 238).

While the optimal treatment still appears to be psychotherapy coupled with medication, it is the *imagery* and the *creativity* of the artist (both therapist and patient) that we must truly pay attention to. Regardless of whether or not our patients are being treated with pharmaceutical, psychotherapeutic, or alternative methodologies, what the art therapist brings to the stage must operate from the plane of investigation of self, the self-that-is and the self that observes the self-that-is. Without this inquiry, there will be stagnation, no growth, and just an addition to the tide of ineffective, deleterious treatment.

Where to Draw the Line

Much has been written about the fine line between creativity and madness and certainly in my case, I have been faced repeatedly with this question. Initially, when a patient is in a state of dis-ease, it becomes all too easy too pathologize via the diagnosis as well as through the interpretation of the art. In creating a three-generation genogram to visually map the psychosocial and chronological history of a client, it is important to list the "strengths" of the patient. Otherwise, it is easy to form toxic and jaded opinions about the prospective treatment of the client. Unless we look for strengths in the medical and psychosocial histories, we can be trapped in the spiraling mentality of looking at a client's symptoms and diagnostic classification instead of operating from the viewpoint of wellness. I caution the art therapist to beware of this trap, no matter if an incipient student or a seasoned traveler. It is all too easy to fall victim to the danger of "fitting in" to this methodology of treatment. While it is important to understand a client's disease, it is often customary to be swayed by diagnostic indicators and definition both in expectation for course of treatment and expected outcome, thus contributing to failure. In the *Power Tactics of Jesus Christ and Other Essays*, the famous family therapist, Jay Haley warns about this in rather ascorbic tongue: "One can say that a patient is … impulse ridden. No therapeutic interventions can be formulated with this kind of language. For more examples of how to phrase a diagnosis so that a therapist is incapacitated, the reader is referred to *The American Psychiatric Association Diagnostic Manual*" (1986, p. 84).

Clearly, Haley is forewarning the therapist (fundamental or experienced) to beware the pitfalls in this stunningly sarcastic article entitled, "The Art of Being a Failure as a Therapist." He ends this trenchant article with the suggestion that every institute that is in the business of training therapists have the following motto on the walls:

Be passive
Be inactive
Be reflective
Be silent
Beware. (1986, p. 88)

Elemental Play and Creativity

Curiosity. Excitement. Concentration. Pride. Joy. We understand that effective learning is driven by these emotions. We also understand that children learn best when they construct something that they find personally meaningful–be it a robot, a poem, a sandcastle, or a computer program. Our products are designed on the belief that children can't be given knowledge; they must actively build their own theories and marry new information to their existing views. There is no single "right answer" to any given challenge, nor is there a single right method to find a solution. The child develops the solution that she feels is best. Learning with LEGO Dacta is based on construction rather than instruction.

http://www.lego.com/learn/about/learning.html
(from the Lego web page)

The reason we have thumbs: Construction. Edifices. Building. Edith Kramer (1975) has referred to construction as one of the highest forms of sublimation. And truly this need to build and create shelter is at the cornerstone of survival. It exists in all strata of the animal kingdom and for humankind, it has gone way beyond the need to merely care for the human nucleus. While I am not about to wax poetically about the environmental indignities that humankind has thrust upon the world, suffice it to say, that as a people, in making life more efficient, we have poisoned our planet in the process. While I love having a washer and dryer in my home and all of the amenities of living in the (almost) twenty-first century (including this wondrous laptop which taps out my babbling), humankind seems to have lost sight of the initial concept of merely "providing shelter." But we are an evolving people. And the edification that is presently ongoing seems to be a part of our greater purpose, that is changing, evolving, adapting, growing, in short, creating. And while we all do it in myriad ways, whether it be an artist molding a sculpture or a business executive resolving a corporate crisis, according to Levinthal (1988), this act taps "not only into the creative enterprise but into any activity for which there is a sensation of total involvement." This is what Csikszentmihalyi (1995) refers to as the "flow experience." He goes on to say:

> . . . in the human mind, meeting difficult challenges became genetically linked with a form of pleasure. Just as we have learned to enjoy what is necessary to survive and preserve the species, like eating and sex, so we might have learned to enjoy the flow experience, which spurs us to master increasingly complex challenges. This *cor irrequietus*, this Faustian engine, could be the source of what we count as human progress. (p. 191)

What Moon (1996) has called "creative immersion" Csikszentmihalyi (1995) refers to as the "flow." As early as 1962, a prominent psychologist, Jerome Bruner, labeled this state of creativity as "effective surprise." He stated:

> . . . It is the unexpected that strikes one with wonderment or astonishment. What is curious about effective surprise, is that it need not be rare or infrequent or bizarre and is often none of these things. Effective surprises . . . seem rather to have the quality of obviousness about them when they occur, producing a shock of recognition following which there is no longer astonishment.

Levinthal (1988) further clarified that through "effective surprise" there is: ". . . a new placement, perhaps merely a rearrangement, that yields in the end a new perspective, so that we can be transported beyond the everyday ways of experiencing the world. As a result, the world is changed, never to be quite the same again" (p. 191).

It has also been suggested that during this state there is a temporary loss of ego and often we ignore the cries of our body for sleep, food, or drink. Instead, we can get caught up in the more celebratory aspects of the work. Of course, this state of euphoria has a flip side to it: depression. Take Alexander the Great who, according to history, wept at the end of his conquests because he felt there were no more worlds to conquer.

Personally, I can attest to and acknowledge that euphoric state. Oftentimes, when I am totally immersed in the writing process, hours can go by in a blink and I not only haven't noticed the time change, but more often than not, I haven't even stirred for that second cup of coffee or made a trip to the bathroom. One day during the throws of a glorious writing weekend at my family compound in the Adirondacks, I sat down with my morning coffee and trusty laptop. My sister ambled by some six hours later and remarked that she was amazed at my level of concentration since I had been sitting there beyond lunch and into the mid-afternoon. Naturally, this broke my concentration and I took a swimming break. But the point is, when I am happily immersed in the "flow," "creative immersion" or "effective surprise," no matter what you call it, for all intents and purposes, I am quite literally in another state. So perhaps I would typify this state of being as *elemental play* that is authentic to the inner creative state. For me, this state of satisfaction is no different than the pleasure derived from food, sex, or any of the other bodily needs. Perhaps that is why the state is so highly addictive. As Levinthal (1988) suggests: "The similarities to drug addiction may be only suggestive and the evidence circumstantial, but nevertheless, it is plausible that we are dealing with the functioning of brain endorphins . . . the endorphins system in the brain have succeeded in allowing the emergence of a peculiarly human attribute: the pleasure of creating something new" (p. 194-195).

Moreover, functioning in this "think tank" condition amongst others produces a certain amount of playfulness. Laughter resounds from the creative sanctum. Levinthal reported (1988) that Lewis Thomas had also spoken about this experience when describing the precipice of a scientific breakthrough. He noted that he could always determine that an important breakthrough was about to occur when he heard peals of laughter coming from the laboratory and people bandied about "preposterous" theories. Levinthal (1988) goes so far as to suggest that as a species we have in fact been ill named. He gingerly suggests replacing the term *Homo sapiens* (which translates into Latin as "the wise one") to the more accurate *Homo ludens* (which means "the one who plays"). Hammer (1990) would most likely agree wholeheartedly to this idea of *Homo ludens* since he is a major proponent of incorporating laughter and humor into the therapeutic arena.

Sweet (1990), in discussing the characteristics of shamanistic writing, writes determinedly about creativity in such a forthright manner that donning sunglasses is practically prerequisite. In unearthing what one needs to *most* write about, he advises:

> . . . make a list of cultural taboos, find one that personally makes you sweat the most - ones that you've repeatedly dreamed about night and day–and then assume yourself sufficiently energized to explore that tension. Writing, after all, is a form of ripping, exposing, revealing, of exorcising what one's particular society and what one's particular self has trouble forbidding. (p. 21)

I might add that digging into these creative trenches is absolutely essential in dusting the critic off of one's shoulders. Otherwise the *elemental* state is compromised and is anything *but* authentic. There is plenty of time to return to the work and play critic, but in order to genuinely allow for *elemental play*, one needs to be a conduit or as Moon (1996) so beautifully expressed, "an imageorator." Beyond shamanistic writing is the capacity to follow such dictum as suggested by Moon. What a perfectly brilliant concept: this would really be following the proverbs of Marshall McCluhan's theory of the "the medium as messenger." But the medium is the taskmaster. The difficulty lies not in the message bearer but in the receiver. In order to enfold *elemental play*, one must be art: otherwise the message is recursive and ill received: thus the term "return to self." So the concept behind *elemental play* is that of circularity–completing the loop within self. And as Sherlock Holmes would say, "It's really quite elemental, my dear."

The concept of elemental play simply allows the art to be the healing agent. It is a powerful and medicinal agent as can be seen in the case presented herein. I know that the evocative power of art can transcend a powerful antidote and contribute toward the wellness of another person's soul. In the case which I present next, the healing power of art is what endeared this young boy and moved him toward the trajectory of self-esteem, self-worth, and recovery. While some might argue the case, I was merely the messenger-orator. Nothing more, nothing less. It was the art that became the catalyst for healing.

CASE ONE: YOU GOTTA HAVE ART

Referring Symptoms: Psychosocial and Medical History (Hx)

Many years ago, in my first job post graduate school, I was working with a variety of emotionally disturbed kids from preschool age through adolescence and their families. One of the children who crossed my path was Randy, a handsome African-American boy aged 11. His social worker and therapist, Mr. M., who stated that Randy had made no gains for two years in traditional verbal psychotherapy, had referred him. Since I had just been hired there, it was decided that I could try and aid this electively mute individual, and assist him toward the ultimate goal of relating verbally to his therapist.

A genogram complete with timeline reveals the nodal events but in a nutshell: Randy had an older brother who had gone off to serve the armed services and essentially, he was left to care-take his mother, who had been divorced from Randy's father since his age 2. Of interest is the fact that his mother abandoned Randy at age 2 and left him in the care of his maternal grandmother until the age of four. At the tender age of six years old, in a barroom, Randy witnessed his father bludgeoned to death by a woman wielding a baseball bat. Pretty horrid stuff. Randy stopped talking from that moment on.

While his mother had remarried, her spouse died approximately one year before I began seeing Randy (his age 10). While the father's murder and the death of his stepfather had understandably traumatized him, subsequently thereafter, his mother's increasing reliance on him preoccupied the team since he had begun sharing a bed with his mother. Moreover, it was reported that Randy and his mother were symbiotically locked in a nurturing-caretaker relationship where more often than not, it was Randy who was the caretaker/nurturer and the mother was protected. For example, the mother reported having bouts of migraine headaches. When she experienced these, she became incapacitated and often Randy would feed her while she rested in bed. As well, the mother only left the house for necessities such as food shopping (and thus began her rapid ascent into an increased 75 poundage) and a daily retreat into reading scripture. The day would be passed ruminating about Randy's problems, eating incessantly, and watching soap operas and such sitcoms on television.

Medically, Randy had experienced myriad ear infections and at age 10 and 11 he had two mastoidectomy operations. While his left ear had normal hearing, he had total sensorineural loss in his right ear.

While there were no reports of behavioral problems in the home, the contrary was reported from the school: it was recorded that he "set up" classmates against each other and his behavior was described as "defiant, negativistic, and controlling." Academically, he functioned well below grade level (approximately two years), yet he excelled in art and recreational activities.

By the time he came to his first art therapy appointment, Randy was still refusing to talk in psychotherapy but was talking in other arenas such as with school and friends. Nevertheless, there was no carryover of this activity in his verbal psychotherapy. And thus, the hopes were that there would be some transference of this activity onto the art and then eventually back to this primary therapist, Mr. M.

The Sessions

The Diagnostic: First Session

Randy arrived to the first session angrily espousing that he had not been informed about art therapy and that he didn't want to attend. (Those were **not** the days of consumer input and I had mistakenly thought the social worker had inquired as to how he felt about this new modality, art therapy. In hindsight, this whole diatribe could have been avoided if either his therapist or I had, in fact, discussed the options with him prior to the first appointment. Big mistake.) I discussed his anger regarding his lack of consent. I explained that he had been referred because he had been refusing to talk

Randy's Genogrammatic Timeline

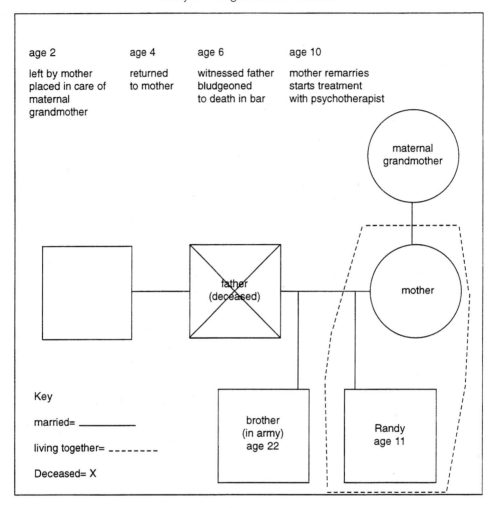

with his therapist, Mr. M. When I assured him that we could use art materials and not talk, he immediately softened, and decided to begin.

I asked him to draw whatever he wanted based on the teaching of Roberta Shoemaker who highlights the significance of the first picture in her well-known article (1977). His first art work, Figure 17, is a picture of a tree. At the risk of being diagnostic and posturing "imagicide," I felt compelled to look at the piece and based on theorists past-read, I describe it as I saw it then and as I see it now some 17 years later:

Then and Now

The typical wide-based stance according to Hammer (1975) suggests over-ly dependent posture within the family constellation and the paper-based

Figure 17.

tree explicates insecurity and feelings of inferiority, while the lack of root system was a dead giveaway and needs no interpretation. But, the interesting point was the one at which he abandoned the drawing of the tree, repeated erasures of the left side of the blossom area.

According to my well-documented notes, I couldn't help thinking about the bludgeoning that he had witnessed as a child. Then my eyes lighted down to the knothole, reported by many (Hammer, 1975; Buck, 1987) to be the age of onset for the seat of trauma, and according to this one, the knothole placed him squarely between the ages of 6-9 (with the age being determined from the root area, mean onset age 0, to the very top of the trunk, mean age onset being present day of client). And at that moment, I realized what was causing him such discomfort to become so ill at ease with the drawing. His response was to brush the artwork against the wall in an act that underscored his low self worth and inability to honor the sacred in his art. According to my notes, I had written about my uncomfortability with how casually Randy treated or shall I say mistreated his artwork from the work in session to denigration of the feelings that followed.

Clearly my own countertransference issues had been set ablaze even in Session 1. This was going to be a long road ahead for both of us. I have found though when something gets pushed in my recesses that there is a reason for this resonation. Hammer (1990) coined this "empathic relatedness" with the client and conjectured that without such relation, work would be void, albeit empty. I would heartily concur with this positioning and further advocate that without this arrangement, a relationship cannot be born entrance and no toil will be administered. Perhaps it could be called lack of labor, lack of love. Or maybe the ironclad words blazoned over the concentration camps entryways, "Arbeit macht frei" (Work makes you free), truly have some application here. I have stated (Horovitz-Darby, 1992) that when looking at countertransference: ". . . analytic neutrality' is a mythological position of which I am clearly incapable. And that is because alas, I am human" (p. 389).

At the risk of sounding redundant, let me put it another way: "Countertransference, analytically speaking, has traditionally been couched as a forsaken wasteland, mired in mistakes and ridden with guilt. However, on another level, it is in fact a gift, a reminder to all therapists that we are merely human" (Horovitz-Darby, 1992, p. 379.).

I didn't know it at the time I wrote my notes, but I know it now, what I was embarking on was transmission to the soul, his and mine.

So, all told, we had 47 sessions together and within that time, I followed Randy's transformation into a budding artist, secured a scholarship for him to attend art classes at the local gallery, and watched this young boy blossom and grow. Considering how constrained his next picture was (Figure 18), the growth is even more pointed.

In the next session, Randy asked me to draw a portrait of him, (which I did), abandoned the previous drawing and instead created a similar tree, only this time, the scrawled blossom was contained within the shaded mass of the tree blossom. Moreover, apples had been added. The part that caused him difficulty was the people. Again, no surprise, especially since he request-

Figure 18. *Tree Blossoming with People.*

ed that I draw his portrait, but unlike most kids who become frustrated at that point, Randy asked for assistance and truly wanted to learn the craft of drawing what was in front of him.

And learn he did. This departure into *elemental play*, where symptomatology falls victim to the creative process is what moves one towards wellness. And the immersion becomes so compelling, so positively healing in its aim, that the urge to stay within that current becomes, if you will, life sustaining, almost like oxygen to the unconscious. *Elemental play* is what drove this case into wellness. A simple place to retreat where the point of analysis hinges on the self and the circularity becomes a self-generative, reparative process. What follows is the details of how this work began, that is when Randy discovered himself and his art.

Time for Art

The third time that we met, Randy announced his desire to have me show him how to draw people. We went back to my office in search of books and he chose a book of Cezanne's work. I showed him the trick of breaking up the picture into quadrants and he captured Paul Cezanne's self-portrait so astoundingly well that it superseded the original drawing that Cezanne did of himself (Figure 19).

Soon thereafter, I had encouraged him to create from still life or his imagination, but he disbanded the prospects, finding protection and comfort in copying the work of others. (His first still life had been going along swim-

Figure 19. *Cezanne's Self Portrait.*

mingly until he attempted to draft the cucumber. Perhaps its phallic-like cucumber precluded him from finishing the piece. Since it wasn't really discussed, due to his mounting anxiety, it was cast aside and later placed in his portfolio (see Figure 20).

It was my mistake to push him towards real life images (via the still life). He was nowhere ready for that. So from that point on, I learned to take my cues from Randy and followed his lead and pace. In the words of Fraenkel

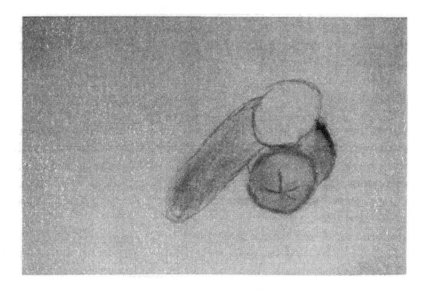

Figure 20. *Still Life.*

(1997), I learned "not to move too quickly" through the process and instead allowed the real work to begin.

Moving slowly through the pain truly allows for the work of reclaiming to begin. Reclaiming the soul is a visionary process guided entirely by the person recovering this lost item. Oh, we therapists can dip and proffer, suggest, and very possibly amend, but the real work needs to come from within the person involved in the process. While there are even shamanistic methods to employ the reclaiming of the souls (such as Waya (1992) describes in the treatise *Soul Recovery and Extraction*), the business of recovering one's soul seems to be a lifelong process. In the instance of time-limited work with patients, sometimes the urgency appears greater. It is then that the therapist, once again, has slipped into the abyss of countertransference and is being led by preconceived notions of aiming one's blocked clients towards health, be it by verbal interpretation or pushing the wrong art materials (as in this case). The necessity of pacing oneself according to the steam of the patient and *not* the institution is the real lesson here. As Joseph Campbell stated in "The Power of Myth," a six-part series broadcast on public television, "The nature of life itself has to be realized in the acts of life."

By our eighth session, Randy had been avidly sharing his artwork with others but quite disparaged one day, he admitted "no one believed" he had made the art. I suggested that as he continued to churn out his work, they would have to come to believe him. Figure 21, a lovely copy of a woman, is representative of his work at this time. While she was a simulated image, Randy had begun to personalize his subjects and the need to reproduce near-perfect representation had finally given way to self-expression. Facial expressions were changed and body postures and garbs were often differently delineated. Clearly her saddened facial cast and half-naked body bares the condition of Randy's mental state at that time. Even her coiffure, befit with a feathered headdress, seemed to put a lid on what was brewing underneath those somber eyes.

It seemed predictable that in the next few weeks, a period of resistance would set in. After all, this business of moving towards wellness is a difficult

Figure 21. *Lady with a Feathered Hat.*

position indeed. For some, it is easier to remain sick than move towards wellness. For that would imply change and change involves growth. Growth, as we know, both physiologically and psychologically can cause great pain. Given the fact that most people operate from the pleasure principle, moving toward the trajectory of change as opposed to stagnation not only takes great aim but courage. And movement towards wellness always entails a certain amount of approach-avoidance. Thus resistance has its place. For many, it is too difficult to aim towards continual growth; the risk is too great—that is losing one's previous operational position and meandering toward the unknown, change. I should have second-guessed that this would come to pass from the expression of those telling eyes in Figure 22. But, I didn't. The old approach-avoidance tap dance had begun. He would miss sessions or retreat into banal, stereotypical work such as writing his name with his mother's sandwiched between his. While this in itself was rather telling, there was an enormous sense of depression that evidenced itself during these times.

Figure 22. *Old Woman.*

For example, one day, Randy entered late to session (per usual) and after a period of name writing he announced that he had a "headache." He disbanded a painting of a girl that he had started. Since Randy had again disbanded a project, and wanted to keep it a "secret" from others, the time for interpretation felt right and so during this session, the conversation went like this:

R: Sorry, I am late again.

E: Uh-huh.

R: I can't work on that picture, it's too big.

E: Maybe we could cut the paper down.

R: No, I don't want to work on it anymore and I don't want to show it to anyone. Let's keep it a secret.

E: A secret?

R: Yes. A secret. *(He made a mistake on the picture.)* I have a headache.

E: Oh Randy, you always say that. Do you know when you say that?

R: When I come out of Gym?

E: Yes, but something else happens when you are tired, or have a headache.

R: When I draw?

E: Yes, but something happens when you draw that makes you "tired" or have a "headache."

R: I make a mistake?

E: Yes. Is it so hard to be imperfect? Is it really so terrible to make mistakes? Everyone makes mistakes.

R: He smiled and looked down at his paper. Can we continue next week?

This was a difficult period for Randy in many ways but what had not been articulated during that session or the one thereafter was Randy's increasing anxiety about his three-week vacation from day treatment and from me. It was not surprising when post vacation, he arrived 20 minutes late. So when he returned from his three week hiatus and told me that he wasn't staying because he had plans to go to "arts and crafts and fool around" with another kid, I suggested that he was avoiding therapy. He countered, "But, all I do is draw." I simply stated, "But that *is* therapy for you, Randy." He began to cry. The truth is often rather potent medicine. So I wasn't at all surprised when he skipped the next session.

Even more eloquent than the artwork of Figure 22 was the work that followed that interpretative session.

The Artist Within

During this stage of Randy's art therapy, he truly connected with the healing properties of the art materials. In an absolutely glorious acrylic painting of a woman, Randy captured a sadness and eloquence that had previously been untapped. In this painting, Randy discovered his joy as an artist. Often, he worked overtime until satisfied with its completion.

This even gave him the courage to pull out the disbanded painting of the girl. Figure 23 below, he aptly referred to as the "*Lady in Red.*" This rendition of a nurse (originally clad in white) had been painted in siren engine red and looked more like a hooker than a healer.

He had invested much time and energy into this painting and talked about wanting to give this to his mother for a Christmas gift. This change in attitude led to renewed interest in the art materials. I spent much time showing him how to blend colors and work with saturation and hue. The result was increased concentration in his work, arriving to therapy on time, requesting additional art training outside of our time together, as well as his request for supplementary art therapy sessions.

I was able to secure a scholarship for Randy at the Memorial Art Gallery and he attended Saturday art classes. After discussion with the team, twice a week art therapy began, approximately nine months into the treatment process. He began signing his pictures and like great artists, who had gone before him, he began titling his work. "*Lady in Red*" was his first titled work.

Positive transference continued at a steady pace, as Randy became more adept and invested in the art process. Verbalization had increased with his mother's caseworker, with his educational therapist, and with me. By default, the team decided that I should become the "primary therapist" and Mr. M. transferred the case. Randy seemed comfortable with this decision and related more openly.

His next painting, again chosen from an image in an art book, was titled "*The Girl in the Room.*" This painting was finished just before his scholarship

Figure 23. *Lady in Red.*

from the gallery kicked in. He was extraordinarily proud of the work and eventually gave it to the Day Treatment program before he was transferred to Outpatient Treatment. Dissanayake (1992) commented on the fundamental human impulse to: "display, share, bestow, and exchange gifts, suggesting that these activities were all part of one social-behavioral complex . . . when gifts are given, offerings made . . . they are made special, arranged to show their sumptuousness and beauty" (p. 107). His increased need to give his work to others may have reflected his unconditional desire for acceptance but somehow it spoke more to the reasons outlined by Dissanayake. Nevertheless, he seemed a tad hypervigilant during this time, understandably so, given all the changes in his life. But when I clarified that the art scholarship was *in addition* to his art therapy, he seemed to relax.

It was during this point in treatment that Randy was able to openly discuss his resentment towards his mother's caseworker, calling her "stupid" and bit-

Figure 24. *The Girl in the Room.*

terly complaining that the caseworker had suggested that Randy stop calling his mother "Peach" and his maternal grandmother "Pie" and instead call them "mother" and "grandma" (respectively). Even when I gingerly interpreted that their pet names reminded me of food (and thus attempted to stir up some of the dependency issues), Randy failed to grasp the importance behind referring to his mother and grandmother in less oral ways. Around this time, his educational therapist, "Ann," was on maternity leave and R's anxiety was at an all time high. In his next pastel painting (Figure 25), he unwittingly substituted Ann's face for that of the model in the book. The resemblance was incredibly uncanny and everyone remarked on the likeness but interestingly enough, Randy just "didn't see it."

Randy was also able to admit that often he would get "sick" and couldn't attend the art classes at the gallery. He expressed embarrassment about telling me and admitted that he feared that I would be "disappointed" in him. (I had suddenly become the critic perched on his shoulder.) Moreover, in the weeks that passed, it became abundantly clear that there was more to his "missing" art classes on the weekends. Randy explained that he felt inadequate compared to his other classmates and in fact this was reflected in his

Figure 25. *Woman and Tree.*

work with me. He would reproach his work and efforts during our session. While his work became increasingly more skilled, his sense of self-worth seemed to plummet. In time, I learned the reason behind these remarks: Randy was frightened that once he left day treatment that our time together would also end. It was decided that I would see him in outpatient therapy in order to allay his concern. Once that was settled, Randy was able to return to his artwork and do increasingly mature work. Figure 26, created during this time, is a beautiful watercolor that Randy set up of fruit and a paintbrush.

A series of eloquent watercolor works followed and Randy's self-esteem increased and his work with the materials reflected his artistic prowess and increased maturation and gratification when working in art. Two beautiful paintings, a landscape, Figure 27, and a seascape, Figure 28, are indicative of his work during this period.

Figure 26. *Still Life.*

Figure 27. *Landscape.*

Figure 28. *Seascape.*

His last work, however, (Figure 29), a watercolor that truly resembled his house appeared to be developmentally regressed and agitated in quality. Randy actually stated that it seemed to be a "scary" house. Many qualities from the blackened windows and doorway, to the crumbling wall structure, bespoke Randy's anxiety about his leaving day treatment.

As well, additional pressure had been placed on his discharge since he had received a "full-scholarship" to attend a technical school because of his artistic talent. While he left confident about continuing in art therapy treatment during this transitional period, his mother canceled his appointments and thus, the outpatient therapy was abandoned. While this saddened me, in my heart, I knew that the outcome was beyond my control and hopefully the art had given Randy the reservoir that he needed.

Years later, I learned that I had guessed right. Ten years had passed since I had seen Randy, placing him at age 22. I never thought that I would pass him in the hallways of the city school district. (I was there because I had been hired to train Special Education teachers in techniques they could use in the classroom.) I was sitting on a bench, waiting to meet with administrative officials and suddenly this tall, handsome, muscular young man passed me. I must have done a double take because he struck me to the core. He stopped, perhaps because either he had caught my stare or had similar shock waves go through him. This handsome man turned on his heel, looked at me, and said, "Ellen? Is that you?"

Figure 29. *Scary House.*

All too quickly, I realized who this young man was and we both connected for a rare follow-up. It turned out that Randy had finished technical college, had majored in photography and art, and had been hired as an art
teacher in the city school district. He was there filling out the necessary documentation. He said that when he had been discharged that he wanted to
come and see me but his mother had refused to take him to treatment. I told
him that I was aware of his mother's decision but had been bound not to
interfere with her decree. Randy explained that while initially he blamed me,
he soon came to realize that it was not my fault. He thanked me for our work
together and most of all for giving him this gift of "art." Randy had truly
taken from our sessions the importance of *elemental play* and had continued
to use it through his life. It was a lovely story of how the art for him had *truly*
made the difference. While I have experienced the evocative powers of art
in my own healing, here was an instance were the materials evoked that
same creative immersion in another human being but in this case, the impact
was not only restorative and life enhancing but perhaps even lifesaving. In
the words of Dissanayake:

> . . . making important activities special has been basic and fundamental to
> human evolution and existence, and . . . while making special is not strickly
> speaking in all cases art, it is true that art is always an instance of making spe-
> cial. To understand art in the broadest sense, then, as a human proclivity, is to
> trace its origin to making special, and I will argue that making special was often
> inseparable from and intrinsically necessary to the control of the material con-
> ditions of subsistence that allowed humans to survive. (1992, p. 92)

It's not the go, it's the way.

ANONYMOUS

Chapter 3

WHEN ART IS ENOUGH

This chapter is a story about possibilities. It is also a message about *paying attention* to what is important. It is so very easy to miss the simple solutions. Unfortunately, I think that this comes from adaptation to a culture that bombards us with stimuli and in turn causes us to tune out energy.

The tale which follows embraces the concept of tuning into another person's energy; in this case, that of a talented and misunderstood ten year old boy. It is a metaphor about paying attention to the most simple and obvious conclusion. As a clinician, this is vitally important: that is truly attending to another and (concomitantly oneself) and one's reactions to any situation. This is not always easy to do. Often, I overlook the obvious and become entrapped by the "solution" and do not heed the "*soulution*" as I have come to see it. In seeing the "*soulution*" of a human being, I allow my energy to mix with the other. This is not about loss of boundaries but rather it is co-creating, connecting/"*kinecting*" and permitting the flow of elemental play to enter the heart and soul of the therapy. Thus, this mixing of forces becomes the "*soulution.*" And in this, I am not the healing agent but rather a participant in wellness: mine as well as the other person's.

It is a double-edged procedure. For in the healing process, whether guiding or receiving the healing energy, *it is not either/or, it is both/and.* One can *not* avoid being affected. Indeed, this process of healing the energy system of a human being is participatory by default. To deny this position is to deny one's existence, one's energy, and the universal constructs of energy itself. We are not inert matter. We mix. Whether for better or worse, this is indeed what we do. In receiving this truth, we can change ourselves, others, and yes, perhaps even the world.

Brian

This is a story generated by paradox. There have been several ironical connections to this tale. I will relay three.

PARADOX ONE (THE RECENT PAST): The first irony occurred approximately a year ago. I was sitting in my office at Hillside Children's Center where I

Figure 30. *The Parting Gift from Brian.* Pleistocene, 3 in. x 2 in.

have been employed for over 15 years. Oddly enough, I had been holding a Pleistocene sculpture that Brian had made for me approximately 12 years ago.

I had just begun researching this book and I was pondering how unfortunate it was that I had never been able to obtain a signed art therapy release form from Brian. I had been thinking what a wonderful illustration this case had been in utilizing a studio art therapy approach.

The phone rang. It was a teacher from the campus school connected to our residential treatment facility. She asked me if I remembered working with a boy by Brian's name. My heart leaped into my throat as I barely eked out, "Why, yes." She explained that he had just phoned the school and asked if he might come and speak to the students at the school since he wanted to "give back" a little something based on what he had received when in treatment with me. She then added that he would be coming that Friday and wanted to know if I would be willing to see him. My mouth dropped as I told the teacher what I was holding and what I had just been thinking. I affirmed that I would be there on Friday.

On Friday afternoon, I entered the room. I barely recognized Brian. He sported at least 6'2" to my 5'2" frame and besides his soft, beautiful blue eyes and wry smile, what I recognized most were his hands: these hands that I had watched for over a year had seared an indelible mark in my memory. His hands were as familiar as 12 years ago. As I approached him, not knowing whether to shake his hand or warmly embrace him, a desk was physically stationed between us. I leaned over the desk as did he, and we embraced. I uncovered the carefully wrapped Pleistocene figure that I had kept on my desk for years and watched as he was shocked back into our time together. He had forgotten about this figure and its presence threw us back 12 years. Quickly, we switched gears as he told me that he had watched the video-movie that we had made together and he then showed me his current portfolio and incredible puppets. I was amazed at his artistic prowess.

I experienced a rare follow-up opportunity with Brian. We conversed freely: artist to artist. Brian had done well. He had received several scholarships for his artistic aptitude after our therapy ended. Indeed, he had been an enormous success, receiving a full scholarship to the prestigious Art Institute of Pittsburgh. Thus began a rare friendship born from a relationship informed by art. While the details of our reconnection, a look at Brian's current art work, and his thoughts on what art means to him will follow the tale of our prior work together, the coincidences involving this case continues.

PARADOX TWO (THE PAST): It is a rare occasion to be a recipient of one's own work. Over 20 years ago, when I was a graduate student in the field of Art Therapy, I became actively involved in NYATA (the New York Art Therapy Association) and read countless legislative bills that were being circulated around Albany. In one such bill, our legislative lobbyist (Pat Lynch) asked the members of NYATA to write rationales for introducing the creative arts therapies into the applicable bills that were being generated. One of these bills was an amendment to Public Law 94-142 in which creative art therapists (art, music and/or dance therapists) could be included in a parenthetical description of "support services." Pat submitted my very simplistic rewrite of that particular bill which was then ratified and amended into law. This created a civil service line for creative art therapists in New York State. In the ratified bill, if a student's IEP (Individualized Educational Plan) was named as a "support service" then, by law, the school was required to fund and deliver that service (Horovitz, 1980; Goodman & Wilson, 1980).

Much to my surprise, in 1983, I became a recipient of my own work in the case of Brian. Brian's school psychologist recognized his aptitude for art and as a result his teacher made an art therapy referral on his IEP. As a result, even though he lived 45 minutes from Rochester, New York, once a week he was bused from his school to my outpatient office for art therapy. We worked together for one and a half years and with school vacations and summer breaks, there was a total of 39 sessions.

The referral on his IEP Phase I (submitted by his teacher) read as follows: "With the recommendation of the school psychologist, an art therapist will hopefully be provided for Brian (Author's Note: named changed for confidentiality). He seems to be able to express himself the best through drawing and since the therapist's approach is to work with the entire family, this should help Brian with his emotions. Her name is Ellen Horovitz and she is willing to see Brian and his family in her office on a weekly basis."

This case referral took place approximately 12 years ago. In those days, the school supplied insufficient psychosocial information to construct a family genogram. What was known was that one of the older sisters and Brian both had learning disabilities, mother and father were both high school graduates, and father had difficulty with language, reading, and numerical computation. It was suggested that there was a genetic predisposition for dyslexia and learning impairment. Father was employed as a truck driver, and mother was employed at the local school cafeteria where Brian and his sister went to school.

Numerous assessments had been done on this 11-year-old child who had been labeled (according to the referring IEP) as "Learning Disabled/ Emotionally Disturbed." On his psychological tests, he scored a Full Scale IQ of 90 on the WISC-R; received an error score of 2 on the Bender Gestalt, which placed him right below age expectancy; received a grade level of 3.0 on the Wide Range Spelling test; and scored a 3.0 on the Woodcock Reading Mastery test. The evaluation upheld that Brian was accurately diagnosed as dyslexic/learning disabled with severe deficiencies in visual-auditory processing. This was reflected in delayed phonetic analysis skills, visual sequencing and reversal problems in reading, retention problems with oral directions and details, and concrete number processing with fingers (indicative of delayed memory/retrieval skills for numeric facts). Psychologically, the school psychologist suggested a severe course of dysthymia (depression) specifically related to school performance and social functioning. Brian was described as having "hypersomnia, low social energy, decreased productivity, decreased concentration, social withdrawal, irritability and/or excessive anger and brooding over the past."

While his diagnoses spanned over the years from age 5- age 11 (when the case was referred), the most inaccurate claim (at his age 7) was from a pediatric neurologist who had diagnosed him as Axis I, Schizophrenia, undifferentiated. This was based on a free drawing of a devil. This one drawing (illustrated during a mental status exam) coupled with Brian's claim of having 'imaginary friends' was enough for the pediatrician to claim this diagnosis. (Personally, I believe that imaginary friends can be a very healthy response to trauma and stress, having had a few imaginary friends of my own.)

I had to put the reports down at this point since I found them preposterous and self-aggrandizing. Nevertheless, his referring symptoms offered a more conclusive picture of what to expect:

a. inappropriate social initiative
b. acting out in nature
c. defensive in nature
d. inappropriate interactions
e. difficulty in monitoring his own behavior
f. reacting negatively to discipline and
g. poor gross and fine motor skills.

Now this last symptom, poor gross and fine motor skills, was a complete surprise since he had been described as having had artistic aptitude. In fact, the initial diagnostic instruments that I conducted disproved this claim of "poor gross and fine motor skills." Brian not only had both talent and creativity, but he also possessed extraordinary skills both two- and three-dimensionally. Following the assessment of the House-Tree-Person Test (HTP) (Hammer, 1980), Kinetic Family Drawing (KFD) (Burns & Kaufman, 1972), the Cognitive Art Therapy Assessment (CATA) (Horovitz-Darby, 1988), and the Silver Drawing Test of Cognition and Emotion (SDT) (Silver, 1996) I drew some rather different conclusions then had been indicated by the psychoeducational reports. This was conducted at Brian's age 11.

The Art Therapy Diagnostic Assessment

Initially, Brian seemed perplexed regarding his referral to art therapy. However, once I explained the testing situation, he became both cooperative and animated. The HTP revealed much interesting information about his family hierarchy and how he felt within the family construct. He defended his "only boy" role and remarked confusedly about whether or not he should be "playing with dolls." His continual verbalization of this point seemed to suggest age appropriate confusion regarding sexual and gender identity conflicts. The verbal associations to this test ranged from harangues about the family constellation to isolated school incidents, which seemed to plague him. His house and tree drawings were finely articulated and well thought-out. His characterization of his person drawing seemed to vividly portray his confusion regarding appropriate roles. He expressed an inability to draw people realistically. This seemed to reflect Brian's difficulty with interpersonal relationships and suggested a tendency towards withdrawal into fantasy.

Figure 31. *Dog on TV.* Drawing from Imagination Subtest, Silver Drawing Test.

On the Silver Drawing Test (SDT), Brian scored in the 99 percent for his grade 5 (with a T score conversion of 76.55). Specifically on the Drawing from Imagination subtest, Brian displayed vivid imagination, sequencing and combining skills.

His clay subtest, Figure 32, is of a troll. His identification with this fantasy character clearly indicated his prowess for imagination. His artistic creations were delightfully refreshing, imaginative, and helped Brian weave fanciful tales and much bravado as projected into his characters' lives. I felt this was a great strength, especially since his classmates constantly teased him and via his characters, Brian was able to act out an alternative vignette. Through his characterizations, Brian had an opportunity to flush out his anger and resentment in a safe, contained, and supportive environment.

Because of his ability to freely associate his inner conflicts regarding familial issues and school-related concerns while working with the art media, I made the following recommendations: monthly family art therapy coupled

Figure 32. CATA, Clay Subtest Troll. 5 in.

with individual weekly art therapy in order to assist Brian in expression of inner conflicts, improve relations with authority figures (both at home and in the school) and provide him with an arena for self expression. Unfortunately, his parents were resistant to involvement in therapy and thus our family work was confined to role-playing, empty chairs and the like as stand-ins for familial members.

According to Lowenfeld and Brittain (1975), the Cognitive Art Therapy Assessment (CATA) reflected Brian to be functioning age appropriately at the Gang Age level of development (age 9-12 years). His troll figure (Figure 32) is a testament to his propensity towards imagination and fantasy; his skills as delineated in the characters are well-developed and entertaining in spirit. I determined nothing bizarre in his responses and all batteries indicated that this young boy had incredible artistic aptitude and would flourish in an educational program specifically tailored for dyslexics. I clearly stated this in my conclusions and even suggested to the Committee on the Handicapped (COH) (now known as the Committee on Special Education (CSE)) that there was a local, nationally recognized (albeit privatized) school (The Norman Howard School) specifically geared toward dyslexic children. But the school would not pay for this education.

PARADOX THREE (PRESENT MOMENT, 12/28/97): As I finished writing up this section, I took a break and made myself a cup of tea. It is always my habit to read through an entire case from the beginning of my notes (the diagnostic) to the end (in this case, all previous reports through Session 39) before picking out the significant data to scribe. I had just finished reading all of the material when the phone rang. It was Brian. I laughed heartily and said, "I just finished reading you." We caught up since we talked last. (Since Brian moved back into the area, we have had regular contact and as an adult he willingly signed a release form for the case and had even agreed to be interviewed and offer his version of how art therapy affected him.) So we talked about the diagnoses (as an adult he had read through all of his files), and his thoughts about the case. Brian had called to give me the number of the school psychologist who first referred the case to me. (Brian had also become a friend with this now retired school psychologist, Norm Davis. I had again met Norm the same day that Brian and I had become reacquainted at Hillside Children's Center. Norm had driven Brian to Hillside Children's Center that day.) Norm conveyed his interest in the book and relayed to Brian that he would be delighted to offer his input. This indeed was a rare opportunity. That is how I have come to view this work and this life that I weave. And was Brian's phoning at the exact moment that I had finished reading the case merely a coincidence? I think not. There are no coincidences, just possibilities.

Significant Sessions

As reported earlier over a period of one and one-half years, there were 39 sessions spanning school vacation breaks (including one summer). By the second meeting (during the diagnostic work-up), Brian was already attaching to me and verbally expressed his sadness regarding his dyslexia. He continually made comments about being "teased" in school and how "sad" this made him feel. He struck me as a very bright, sensitive, artistic child that struggled with a very curable situation, dyslexia. Unfortunately, he had been earmarked at an early age as "disturbed" because of his academic frustration that led to acting out in the classroom. What I found disquieting about this case was that early intervention had turned up inappropriate labels such as schizophrenia instead of being employed for what seemed to be a rather transcendent problem. Frankly, when these kinds of labels are cast on children, I often wonder who is the more disturbed, the clinician or the system. While the answer is neither *either/or but both/and*, it still is disconcerting in its outcome. In my opinion, this boy was distressed by his impairment, but he was traumatized by the responses of both the professionals and children that surrounded him.

By Session Five, it became clear that Brian's modus operandi had been his incredible retreat into fantasy. Because he had been identified as disturbed and learning disabled, he was readily cast as the school "dunce." His only resort was to retreat into drawing, fantasy, and elaborate storytelling. Nevertheless, the art therapy sessions became a haven for this activity. Brian would enter week after week and tell me about being bullied and then with the greatest subliminal aplomb, he would turn this unfortunate incident into artistic gratification.

It became clear to me that involving his parents would be advantageous at this point. So I invited them to come in for a session, but unfortunately they didn't show up. Brian was clearly disappointed as was I. Nevertheless, we trudged on and tried to solve the situation together, often bringing the parents into the room as advisors (e.g., I would make statements like, "What would your father suggest if he were here now?"). This gave us an opportunity to do some role-playing but the issues were expressed by way of acting this out via the art creations that Brian fabricated.

By Session Nine (3 months into treatment), the school reported improvement academically and socially. Unfortunately, Brian's teacher left the following week and this caused a major setback for him. Thankfully, Brian was able to talk about his feelings regarding his teacher leaving. Nevertheless, entrusting his faith in a new teacher would require much time.

By the end of Session 13 (approximately four months into treatment), Brian was still expressing negative feelings about his inability to read well

Figure 33. Troll Characters. Paper and pencil, 12. in x 18 in.

and continued to harbor low self-esteem and depression regarding his inadequacy in these areas. As well, he continually voiced his disappointment regarding his parents not attending sessions. While I repeatedly tried everything from phone contacts to letters to the COH chairperson in order to convey the importance of parental involvement, the parents still refused to come in for treatment. As a result, I felt isolated in the situation and decided to use some educational tactics to help Brian with his dyslexia.

Over the next few weeks we went from tracing cardboard letters of the alphabet to actually making them out of clay. This hands-on tracing/shaping of letters really seemed to aid Brian and his ability to read more accurately improved from this point on. In the interim, he continued to make drawings of trolls as can be seen in Figure 33.

Six months into treatment, I finally met with the mother and the father during a session with Brian. They were willing to come in for "information sharing" but claimed that their work schedules prohibited future attendance of family art therapy sessions. Even though I offered alternative times (evenings, weekend appointments) the response was the same: their schedules precluded future meetings. I thanked them for coming in for the "information sharing session" (obviously a one-time shot) and suggested that we could have regular phone contact. They agreed to the idea and Brian orchestrated the family session by instructing his parents to make characters for his movie. His parents followed Brian's direction extremely well and their interaction clearly conveyed this. Below are the characters that they made which Brian then named "Oriental" (made by father) and "Mr. Droopy" created by Brian's mother. Clearly, their attendance enriched our sessions together as Brian viewed their coming to session as commitment (see Figure 41).

Unfortunately, their inability to come in for future sessions adversely affected Brian since he refused to work on dyslexia exercises until his parents (or at least his mother) came into treatment. At this point, I relayed this information to the school and suggested that they continue to work with Brian's academic struggles while I focused on the emotional issues connected to his depression and underlying anger.

By the eighth month into treatment (Session 21), Brian decided to make an animated movie and form the characters from oil Pleistocene. This was an enormous undertaking, which involved much preparation on both of our parts. As well, it facilitated another way for us to work on his dyslexia without the added pressure of academic rigor: a script was necessary as well as the creation of cards, which sported the names of each character. Over the next four months, all of the characters for the movie were created. They ranged from brutish types (like those that teased him at school) to sweet baby troll characters fashioned with lollipops. Of all the characters created, the one I found most interesting was Grumpy, who, according to Brian, "could change into anything." Only Figures 34 and 35 were created before a two-month summer vacation interrupted our sessions. Yet, when Brian returned for art therapy in autumn (Session 29), he displayed much enthusiasm about getting right back to work on his movie. And so the work continued without incident until October (Session 34). At this time, because Brian was doing so well, it was decided that art therapy would terminate in December. Nevertheless, Brian was angry about the decision not to fund continued art therapy services. Since he had been doing so well, I found it difficult to justify continuing the school-related expense. Brian seemed to have developed the wherewithal to be more productive, less depressed, and had gained ego gratification and maturation from using the art materials. As can be expected, as we progressed towards the end of treatment, Brian became somewhat verbally aggressive towards me. However, as soon as I interpreted what was going on, he calmed and admitted his sadness about termination. Naturally, this brought up guilt and countertransferential feelings in me. On the one hand, I truly enjoyed working with Brian and could certainly understand how continued sessions could only enhance and augment his artistic, academic, and emotional potential. Nevertheless, I also understood the school's position. Clearly, this was a costly endeavor regarding transportation alone: an entire school bus was required to transport Brian back and forth to my sessions (45 minutes from his hometown) and as well, there was the payment to the bus driver as well as my outpatient, private practice fee.

During the last session, we watched the video production together, talked about our work together, and I gave him a copy of the video production. After 39 sessions, which spanned approximately a year and a half, the therapy ended. Brian's dyslexia was not cured but he was now well-armed with his art to use for sublimation and self-expression.

Below are reproductions of Brian's character for his movie. A slight description of each character's personality trait follows:

Figure 34. *Goober.* Oil pleistocene, 5 in. Goober was the character with whom Brian identified and the protagonist of the movie.

Figure 35. *Blockhead.* Oil pleistocene, 5 in. Blockhead could have been a stand-in for how Brian felt about himself since he had been labeled the "class dunce." Blockhead was Goober's foe.

Figure 36. *Smiler*. Oil pleistocene, 5 in. Smiler was a friend of Blockhead's and another enemy of Goober, the protagonist.

Figure 37. *Grump*. Oil pleistocene, 5 in. Grump was another villain in this story and possessed the amazing characteristic of being able to transform into anything.

Figure 38. *Little Snot.* Oil pleistocene, 3 in. Little snot was Goober's younger sister.

Figure 39. *Ace.* Oil pleistocene, 5 in. Ace was the hero that saved Little Snot and aided Goober. While he was red in hue, he bore angelic wings.

Figure 40. *Booger.* Oil pleistocene, 5 in. Goober's older brother.

Figure 41. *Oriental and Mr. Droopy.* Oil pleistocene, 5 in. While these characters were created by Bill's father (Oriental) and mother (Mr. Droopy), Brian gave them names. The relevance of the parental investment vis-a-vis these characters was connected to both their participation in their son's therapy but more importantly, their participation in his wellness.

As can be seen by the above characters, Brian clearly sublimated his fantasies into this art/play/video therapy and extracted much self-esteem through not only their creation but more importantly in the opportunity to work through his feelings in a safe and supportive environment. This opportunity allowed Brian to embrace his creativity and escape into fantasy.

Twelve Years Later

As stated previously, Brian and I reconnected because he initiated the contact and wanted to "give something back" to Hillside children. While he was never placed in residential treatment, even as a child coming to the clinic for outpatient treatment, he empathized with the other residential children in my care. In fact, one of the residents (with whom I worked) made props for Brian's movie. While they never met (because of confidentiality) they certainly admired each other, knew each other intimately through the art works that were on display in my office, and even teamed together in the movie making process, albeit without ever meeting! That itself was an unusual phenomenon. Brian had influenced others and clearly wanted to give back. So I wasn't surprised by the generosity of Brian's offer of meeting the kids at Hillside and displaying his present wares.

His artwork, as demonstrated by the body of work that follows, is extraordinary. Brian is truly a gifted model-maker and is enormously talented both two- and three-dimensionally. It has always been my belief that truly great artists are comfortable in both two- and three-dimensional media. If one looks to the great masters, that theory holds true. Brian holds a genuine gift and as has been demonstrated by his scholastic awards, others also believe this to be true.

Brian's work stands alone and defies interpretation and/or description. It is as legendary as his mind, a testament to the wonders of art and what it can instill in others: wellness, imagination, maturation, gratification, and the salubrious nature that lies within each of us. Below are samples of his current day models and drawings for his ideas.

Figure 42. *Creature.*

Figure 43. *Old Man.*

Figure 44. *Sketches for Models.*

Figure 45. *Final Puppet.*

These few pictures are just a smattering of Brian's astonishing artistic capabilities. Rather than wax on about his skills, I have invited Brian to view what I have written so far. In his own words, Brian has written his "Afterthoughts" about his mislabeling and as well as his feelings about art therapy and how this affected his development as an artist and a human being.

Afterthoughts from Brian

After I read the chapter, there were things that I remembered really well and there were things that I really didn't remember. Actually I can recall the first time, the first session that I met you. I recall the pathway in the back going to your office. I recollect lots of little bits and pieces like the sidewalk . . . walking back there at night. I was very scared, which of course is understandable. I already had had a bad experience with counseling. The whole experience was very strange for me, going up into the city and all; it was all very different.

Everyone tends to focus on the word "therapy" in art therapy and I considered that a frightening word mainly because of my past experiences with therapists and psychologists. I didn't have a lot of really good experiences. There were some really bad ones. You reported the misdiagnoses quite well. One doctor made a stupid statement like, "He doesn't need to read to be a ditch digger," not to mention that this same person made a crystal ball prediction that by the age of 17 I would either be in jail or would have committed suicide. It was just amazing to me, the arrogance that some of these people had. So I tend to look at therapy kind of differently now. I find the whole concept very hard to understand. I feel with everything, whether it's scientific or psychological, that it is all-theoretical. It's an educated guessing game. I am amazed. After an hour with me, because of using some psychological techniques, the doctors felt they knew me well enough to make some of the statements that they did. I found that ridiculous, especially with me, because I really put up quite a front. I created a definite protection, if you will. I watched what I said, what I did, whenever I had any kind of therapy, and I was expecting you to be the same kind of strange person. And you were definitely strange but only because you were an artist.

I remember that when I first came to see you that you were attempting a very technical approach (because you were assessing my skills). I remember the Silver Drawing Test. That one I enjoyed. I had no concept of what you were doing. I thought, "What the Hell is she talking about?" And then I got creative with it and used it as a challenge. That was when I was still trying to figure you out, too. I was trying to figure out what kind of a person you were. As I said, in the past when I had gone into a therapist's office, I really tried to say what I thought they wanted to hear. I remember sitting there talking about my interests. That was one thing I liked about you: you were willing to listen to my interests and you didn't talk down to me about them, as a lot of adults tended to do. But later, I became angry with you that we stopped therapy because the school committee told me that you didn't want to continue the therapy. And once you told me your reasons for terminating therapy I was fine with it, but originally, the committee tried to pin it on you.

When I was seeing you, I remember I was trying to express what I was feeling about school in my drawing . . . it was very grim . . . I wanted to do a whole series of these drawings where the main character was completely nuts. It definitely came from the frustration of being at that school. It really helped to talk to you about it.

I could see what you saw in the Kinetic Family Drawing—some things were dead on and some were off. My psychologist showed me your report when I was working with you. I had two reactions: "You mean she is analyzing my drawings?" and the other was, "Gee, I thought we were just hanging out and doing art together." But then after awhile, I didn't care because I knew that was what your job was. I knew everyone's interpretations were going to be different. You could probably show the Kinetic Family Drawing to another art therapist and her take would be different on it.

So much happened. It was over ten years ago and I think the video definitely helped. It made me focus on a goal. After we completed the video, I wanted to do another one for the longest time. In fact, it kept me working with clay. It did help me. I think that the intervention was timely. There were other things going on at home and school that played a factor but working with you really did help a lot. Getting me to focus in on my stuff helped me to become a more three-dimensional artist. And I am not sure if it helped with my dyslexia but now I rely heavily on researching and reading about the characters before I even create them.

I have learned to adapt to my dyslexia and I started reading very well even when I was seeing you. But I didn't start really reading for research purposes until I was able to buy my own books (approximately age 15). I started out with science fiction and fantasy. Once I had completed *Lord of the Rings*, which was steeped in mythology, I began to research original mythological readings. It was an incredible opening for me, especially the stories that had a folklorist mentality. It is something that I think we have lost. These days, people seem to get all their fantasies from the movies. The original Sleeping Beauty, for example, is a lot darker that what was portrayed in the Disney films. Rapes, cannibalism, were included in these original writings. It was very dark stuff. And this appealed to me.

In the video, while I most identified with the character, "Goober," each one of the characters was a different part of my personality. "Smiler" really came from the attitude of being mystified over being "timed out" at school. The time-out rooms were really horrible. Some of these characters, like Smiler, were my response to this very abusive system. I learned to beat the system. They would send me down to the time-out room for five minutes and I would end up staying there for two hours, sometimes the whole day. I would take a nap on the floor and after awhile they realized that it wasn't an effective punishment for me at all. Other kids would literally flip out in those rooms. The first few times I was placed in one of those rooms, I didn't know how to handle it. The worst of school was that I didn't learn anything when I was there.

When I first started in school, they lost my records and started me over in the same math textbook. It made me feel like an idiot. But you had mentioned the positive relationship that I had with my teacher. Mister, let's call him Mr. Igor, found all kinds of ways to make us interested in what we were learning. He had stories to make us remember things. He was able to stimulate our minds; he was a very cool guy who never abused his power. I don't remember anyone being sent to the time-out room when he was in charge. I finally became really upset about being held back and I told Mr. Igor about it. I wanted to learn. He really pushed me by placing me in a more advanced math class. But then he left and I believe it was because of a disagreement with the school.

The school then sent in this woman who had no patience and that is when the time-out rooms really began to hit. At the same time, that is when I wanted to go into other classrooms (like science). She was with me for the next two years. And this woman placed me back in the old math text. So I had a three-year educational gap. I felt like that school was nothing more than a warehouse of kids that weren't wanted by their home schools. Many of the kids were like me—intelligent, angry, and misdiagnosed. Luckily, I had a good family and counseling with you. The art therapy helped me get through that. It was something I looked forward to, especially when we started doing the video.

Making the video in art therapy really helped me. I can see similarities from the characters in the video to the kids that irked me in the school. There was one kid that used to say these terrible things and "Smiler" came from him. He was bright and funny but extremely weird. He had a little comic book that he made called the "Thing from Hell." There were times that he frightened me. And then there were other characters that came from my own imagination, like "Blockhead." I think that you analyzed him pretty well. He was a representation of how other people saw me. I think that it was that and more. Usually when I built the character it was also other things and other people around me. "Blockhead" was a figure that represented how people saw me but I also represented people that just didn't get it. I saw a lot of that kind of person in the school and it was something that I didn't want to be. This was not for me. I didn't want to be like that. Eighteen, 20 year-olds, still in school had basically become everything that people told them they were going to be. I didn't want to be that way. I did what I had to do to get out of there.

So the video and the story line came out of the top of my head. I knew I wanted someone to be rescued. It turned out to be "Lil Snot" who represented my sister in a lot of ways. Goober, the hero, represented me. But the combination of things and working with the materials and you really helped me a lot. The way that you approached art therapy really helped me a lot. You allowed me to express my fantasies through the story and the art materials. Your approach definitely helped me transcend the difficulties that I experienced in school.

Today as an artist, I make permanent characters via Sculpey and more permanent materials. The idea of permanency helps a lot and now being able to make money from creating these sculptures has enhanced the level of work even more because of the professionalism involved. Some people think I am insane when I am in the throes of creating these characters. Often I speak in the voice of the character, like "I'm blind, give me eyes, let me see." With each sculpture, now often based on literature, my interpretations are quite different than others people's takes on the character.

I work with fantasy now because of the need to escape but it's not to forget reality. I look at it as delving into the human condition because everything is based upon emotion. With each sculpture that I do, each one represents a different aspect of myself or maybe something I would like to be. All my work, in some ways, is a self-portrait.

Conclusion

The afterthoughts were obtained in interview format after Brian had read the chapter. It was wonderful to learn that he liked this section and felt that I had captured much of our time together quite accurately. But of course there were many surprises, like discovering that his school psychologist had shared the results of the art therapy assessment with Brian. Had I been privy to that information, I might have been able to explore his feelings about his frustration with previous therapists as well as his resentment towards me. Moreover, I was unaware that the school had suggested that the termination of the art therapy was my suggestion and thus, I mistook Brian's negative transference towards me as part of the termination process. Again had I known what he was feeling, I might have explored the last stages of our therapy quite differently.

One of the more interesting comments made by Brian about his story line for the video that he created was his admission about the rescue theme of "Lil Snot." While Brian stated that "Lil Snot" was a stand-in for his sister, he concluded his afterthoughts by talking about his work as being a "self-portrait." Considering how trapped he felt in this educational system, it is clear that even "Lil Snot" represented that feminine part of his psyche that demanded delivery from an archaic, educational system. His saving "Lil

Snot" via the characters "Goober, Ace, and Booger" was a testament to his ability to heal himself in the face of what Brian considered to be a primitive, antiquated edification.

In all, it was a gift to discover that my intuition about using a studio-based art therapy approach was the right one for Brian. I often say to my students to remember the gift that they bring that is their art. Art is a powerful, medicinal tool. It is the strongest 'uptake' that we have to unleash the unconscious and aid in the transformation of a human being. We are by nature a creative species. Unlocking that artistic potential is an art therapist's richest resource. In Brian's case, it unleashed his power to become a fuller, happier human being. Brian created because he had to. It was his avenue towards wellness and transformation. It was and continues to be a wellspring of power for him.

Creativity, as a response to nodal events, can truly heal the human condition. As Henry James once said, "We work in the dark, we do what we can. Our doubt is our passion, and our passion is our task. The rest is the madness of art."

. . . once in a dream I saw a snake swallowing its own tail, it swallowed and swallowed until it got halfway round, and there it stopped and there it stayed, it was stuffed with its own self. some fix that.
we only have ourselves to go on, and it's enough.

CHARLES BUKOWSKI
YOU GET SO ALONE AT TIMES IT JUST MAKES SENSE

Chapter 4

PRIMARY PROCESS: GAINS FOR THE ARTIST/THERAPIST

Art, Dreams, and Messages Down Under

Sometimes therapy can take unusual, rather unorthodox twists and turns, like: going to a restaurant with an anorectic client and finding out that she eats only ice cream because anything that she swallows that is "hard" reminds her of forced fellatio with her father; or taking a walk in the woods which we call "walk therapy" in order to clear the liver (third chakra) of the physiological poisons that seem to "contaminate" the mind; or prior to therapy, meeting an agoraphobic patient at the end of a block in order to desensitize her to her world; or conducting a session at a graveyard with a family and minister in order to truly bury a lost one. The stories have been myriad, the results extraordinary. In other words, whatever works is what I do. My therapeutic engagements can often be as unconventional as the canvas that I am painting. And inviting such therapeutic encounters can often produce a varied and unusual tapestry, which defies pattern but not meaning. It is creativity at its highest level this co-creating with another human being. And it is that gift that we have to offer each other in the exchange towards the common goal of health.

I urge the reader to look at the options: as a creative artist/therapist one can choose any medium to allow for such creative activity: poetry, short story personal narratives, Qi Gong, meditation, art, music, dream work or play to name a few. In the next case of Brett, a 13-year-old adolescent boy, I will share how working with dreams, art, nature, meditation, and play have opened this boy's journey. I chose this case for a few reasons:

a. while Brett was an unusually bright child (IQ in the superior range) his artwork did not reflect any extraordinary artistic talent, and

b. this will allow the reader to view the evocative power behind creative art therapy even when the patient is neither talented nor particularly invested in the art materials.

105

c. it is also an opportunity to see how the written word, art, play, meditation, and dreams can be used as an interactive modality with a patient.

First, let's take a look at Brett's psychosocial history:

Psychosocial History

Brett, a handsome, Caucasian 13-year-old boy, was the first child born to
his mother, Janet, and his father, Brett, Sr. in 1984. The history noted that
Brett's father was abusive towards the mother before, during, and after preg-
nancy. As a result, the mother divorced Brett's father when he was two
months of age. She struggled concomitantly with guilt and depression
regarding single parenting. At Brett's age 2, the father was incarcerated for
rape. Once he was released from prison, the father had periodic contact with
Brett. It was reported that at Brett's age three, the father wielded a wet baseball bat and broke Brett's nose in several places. As a result, surgery required
11 hours of reconstructive work. At Brett's age of four (1988), his mother
married her second husband and two more children resulted from this
union. Mother's second husband, Chuck, raised Brett as his own. Brett had
no further contact with his biological father until his age of 11 (1995) when
he went to live with his biological father and the father's girlfriend. The reason for this residential change was reported to be because of Brett's out-of-
control behavior. This arrangement was short-lived since father was incarcerated for armed robbery. The biological father is presently in jail and due
to be released this year and mother has grave concerns regarding this situation. At that time, Billy returned to live with his biological mother, Janet.
When that became unmanageable due to Brett's acting-out behavior, Brett
was referred for residential, emergency placement at Hillside Children's
Center where I worked for the past 15 years.

Educational History

Brett attended regular education until the fourth grade when he was clas-
sified as emotionally disturbed and placed in a 12:1 classroom because of his
aggressiveness. This was later changed to a 6:1:1 (6 children: 1 teacher's
aide: 1 teacher) classroom because of continued oppositional defiance. The
situation deteriorated even further and he was then recommended for Day
Treatment and attended a class with a 4:1:1 (4 children: 1 teacher aide; 1
teacher) ratio and had his own aide 1:1 (1 aide: 1 child). He was continually
physically and verbally abusive to peers and adults, which resulted in school
suspension. He was then referred to Hillside Children's Center and placed
temporarily in the Emergency Program until a bed opened up in the resi-

dential unit. Brett has been residing at the unit since July 1997. He began Art Therapy in November of 1997.

Psychological Testing

Brett is a bright youngster who tested in the superior range for intelligence on the WISC-R (Weschler Intelligence Scale for Children, Revised) with a Full Scale IQ of 120. Yet he scored significantly below his cognitive ability on the WIAT (Wechsler Individual Achievement Test). Some frustration was observed on the PIAT (Peabody Individual Achievement Test) as well as the Bender Visual-Motor Gestalt Test. On the Bender, numerous brain injury indicators were present and were of highly significant frequency and variation. As a result, given the history of physical trauma (age 3) and unprovoked outbursts, it was recommended that further neurological testing be administered.

Brett's Timeline

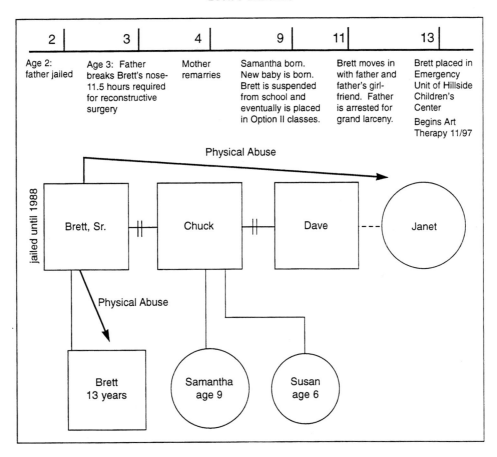

An abbreviated genogram will help elucidate the psychosocial history and parameters of Brett's personality.

Art Therapy Diagnostic Assessment

TEST ADMINISTERED: Cognitive Art Therapy Assessment (CATA) Paint, Clay, and Drawing subtests; Kinetic Family Drawing (KFD); Art Therapy Dream Assessment (ATDA)

Reasons for Referral

Brett was referred by his social worker for the following reasons:

a. To determine whether or not a non-verbal intervention (e.g., art therapy) would aid Brett in appropriate self-expression and serve as a vehicle for appropriate interactions with others.

b. To determine whether or not an art therapy diagnostic assessment could uncover further information about Brett regarding his past abuse.

c. To offer Brett an avenue for non-verbal communication that might translate into increased self-esteem both in and out of the session.

d. To explore psychosocial issues related to his aggressive behavior and past psychosocial issues.

Behavioral Observations

Brett engaged very quickly with me, was extremely cooperative in all of the testing, and was amenable to finishing all of the testing required for the assessment procedure. He seemed quite invested in the materials and was also quite able to make verbal associations to the work produced. During the testing situation, he exhibited no anxiety and was quite relaxed throughout the meetings even when material provoked effect-laden responses.

One of my chief concerns (shared by Brett's social worker) was Brett's propensity for exaggeration. Several times during the testing situations, Brett seemed to communicate inflated information in an attempt to impress me. Perhaps this reflected his unconditional desire for acceptance and nurturance. Given his psychosocial history of domestic violence, his desire to be accepted and cared for seemed understandable and a strength: while Brett has had devastating parental experiences, his capacity to forge new relationships and be vulnerable will stead him well in moving towards a trajectory of health.

Figure 46. Clay Subtest, 8 in. long

Figure 47. *The Monster.* Tempera paint, 12 in. x 18 in.

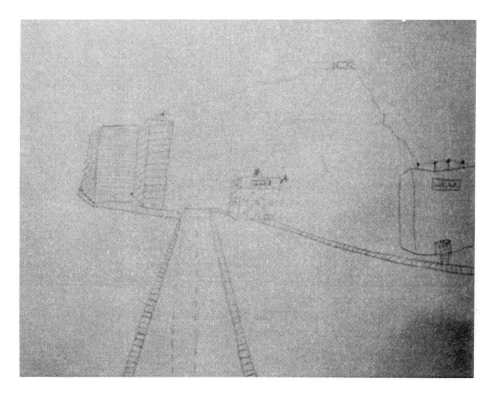

Figure 48. *Communication.* Paper, 12 in. x 18 in.

CATA (Cognitive Art Therapy Assessment)

Brett started with the Clay Subtest and created a canoe with two missals and a palm tree. This unlikely pairing of an object of nature (the palm tree) and aggression (the missals) seems to reflect his ambivalent posture and pairing of nurtuant-related themes to violence. This is not at all surprising given his psychosocial history and need to defend against the feelings associated with the residual recall he has maintained since his childhood abuse.

He tended to exaggerate throughout the sessions and talked about being "spoiled by his grandmother," "wanting to be back home with his family" and "missing his sisters." He also talked about his father and how angry he was with him.

His second subtest, the Painting Subtest revealed more of his true nature and the feelings associated with his inability to protect himself. He created a "monster in a cave" but denied that the monster was himself. It is possible that the monster reflected feelings of inferiority, a concomitant need to defend himself from others, as well as feelings of alienation and isolation regarding the family constellation.

Brett's CATA Drawing Subtest revealed similar themes of isolation and a desire to be connected with others. He created a perspective drawing of a radio tower connected via satellite transmission to a house (unnamed but possibly his from the verbal association) and Kodak office buildings (which are not far from his familial home). The lack of people and emphasis on buildings as a means of communication again seems to reflect his desire for relations (satellite transmission) and simultaneous need to distance relations with people (connection made only to buildings and no visible people represented in the picture). Moreover, Kodak, associated with photography, seems to be yet another symbol for Brett's need to distance himself.

<u>Clay Subtest</u>: Pseudo-Naturalistic Stage of Drawing, Age 12-14 years, Lowenfeld & Brittain.

<u>Painting Subtest:</u> Gang Age, Age 9-12 years, Lowenfeld & Brittain.

<u>Drawing Subtest:</u> Pseudo-Naturalistic Stage of Drawing, Age 12-14 years,

Figure 49. KFD. Paper and pencil, 8 in. x 11. in

Lowenfeld & Brittain.
<u>Overall CATA Score:</u> Pseudo-Naturalistic Stage of Drawing, Age 12-14 years,
Lowenfeld & Brittain, (low end of the spectrum).

Kinetic Family Drawing (KFD)

In the KFD, Brett created a stick figure drawing of his family playing soft-
ball together. His sisters were depicted in the outfield (a revealing metaphor
suggesting his desire to be in the "in" (playing) field and keep his sisters in
the "out" field). He placed himself at bat, and Dave, mother's boyfriend, was
drawn from a rear view, catching. The drawing (done from a bird's eye view
or topographical representation) suggests his need to dissociate around family of origin issues. Despite the fact that the family is viewed doing something
"together," the compartmentalization of all family members as well as the
regressed quality of the drawing (stick-like figures) bespeaks his anxiety
attached to the family constellation. Moreover, Brett's position of being "at
bat" while mother pitches and her boyfriend catches, places Brett literally
between mother and her intended fiancé, definitely a place chock full of
ambivalence for Brett and his mother. This bespeaks the level of competition
that Brett feels in this familial "playing field."

Art Therapy Dream Assessment (ATDA)

Next we did the dream assessment task. After completing a clay sculpture
of a recurring dream that Brett claims to have nightly, I asked Brett to write
a paragraph (script) of the dream. He wrote: "In the scene that I made, a
scorpion, manta ray, and snake are killing me. The snake is always on my
right side and the scorpion always on my left. Then there's the manta ray. It
is always just hovering there. It has a tail like a spear and teeth like daggers."
The next task involves choosing a cluster of statements that really stand
out. They are underlined below: "In the scene that I made, a scorpion,
manta ray, and snake are *killing me*. The snake is *always on my right* side, the
scorpion *always on my left*. Then there's the manta ray. It is always just *hovering there*. It has a *tail like a spear* and *teeth like daggers*." From there the process
involves reducing the clusters even further. He wrote: "killing right, left,
hovering spears, daggers."
The final process requires using the last words to write a complete sentence that sums up the experience. Brett wrote: "There is killing right and
left, there are hovering spears and daggers."
From this statement, I was able to help Brett look at the disparate parts of
himself in the dream and we were able to talk not only about his aggressive

Figure 50. ATDA. Clay at 7 in. x 2 1/2 in.

feelings but the parts of himself that he wants to "kill off." I suggested that we could begin to focus our treatment along these lines. Brett agreed to the work ahead.

Conclusion and Recommendation

Brett is an extremely bright child who relies on a variety of defenses in order to cope with overwhelming feelings of aggression, low self-esteem, and a strong desire for a nurturant, consistent relationship. Cognitively, he seems to be functioning at the low end of the Pseudo-Naturalistic Stage of Development, approximately age 10 years according to Lowenfeld and Brittain. While I believe that Brett can make great strides in individual treatment, I strongly recommended that Family Art Therapy be added as a modality within the next two months in order to accelerate progress and allow for corrective experiences.

Significant Sessions

This is a case illustration where I have used brief, solution-focused therapy in both conventional and uncommon ways. Some of the modalities have included "walk therapy," play therapy, art therapy and psychotherapy techniques. Residential treatment can be as short-lived as a few days to three months. Before the advent of HMO's, the average length of stay used to be one and a half years. While I have always "gone for the jugular," today it is almost compulsory to expedite treatment. While some might insist that one could only administer Band-Aid® therapy under limited confines, I would argue. Since I service the Emergency clinic at Hillside Children's Center, I can attest to the significance of even one session. I have witnessed the ability of one session to produce significant changes in a client. While I prefer long-term treatment, I have seen radical changes in just a few sessions when I truly model and resonate the commitment necessary to stimulate transformation. This has been the case with Brett.

By Session 4, therapy began to occur outside of the office perimeter. Beyond trips to various stores to procure art supplies for varied projects including a birdhouse, we also began to explore the environment, e.g., taking walks in the woods to obtain materials. Of interest was how the walks influenced the dynamics of the therapy sessions. Brett began to talk about issues close to his heart, yet at the same time, his need for bravado guided these walking sessions: Brett needed to exaggerate his experiences and often seemed to puff up like a peacock as he desperately tried to impress me. Confronting his lies was of no avail. Instead, what became necessary was to find a way to weave truisms into the therapeutic context.

What enlisted truth-telling was positive transference. Brett's identification with me was firmly rooted: he even photographed me with his own camera so that he could "have me" over the Christmas vacation. (Talk about a transitional object.) Brett also initiated a much needed hug goodbye before he left for his Christmas vacation. This was Brett's way of pacifying his falsehoods as well as alleviating his anxiety regarding his impending home visit.

By Session 7, I had found an opportunity to address his need to lie: Brett had been returned early from his home visit over the Christmas vacation due to aggressive behavior aimed at his siblings and mother. Nevertheless, when I asked him about his home visit, he denied any problems with the family. During the art therapy session, I suggested that we play with the Lil' Tikes[c] dollhouse in my office. At one point, Brett began to bark like a dog. I had told him that we could have "bark therapy" during art therapy since he was prevented from giving voice to these feelings anywhere else in treatment (e.g., the residential cottage and school). In order to temper his bark, we muzzled the Lil' Tikes[c] boy/dog and then both Brett and his mother and father dolls respectively grew large noses because of their propensity towards lying. They became the Brett-noccio family (like Pinnoccio). This gave me an opportunity to address his lying via the play characters.

The following session was a beautiful sunny January day. Brett had been ill before therapy and had vomited that morning. I felt that it would be salubrious for Brett and I to take a long walk before we began art therapy. Soon after we hit the fresh air, Brett's color changed from pallid white to a blush pink rose. The illness seemed to be clearing. It was evident in his mirthful step and cheerful demeanor. He felt compelled to show off in front of me and demonstrated his aptitude for body surfing on snow and waxed on about his faculty for snow boarding and ice skating. As usual, Brett was performing in peacock fashion, constantly aiming to please and impress me. I did little to neither encourage nor discourage his ritualistic behavior. At one point, we found a grapevine shelter. It was unclear as to whether or not its construction had been formed by animals or humans and we began to add more grapevines to it. Brett crouched down in the created structure and said that he could "live (there) forever and would be happy." This gave me an opportunity to address his feelings about (a) living at Hillside and (b) returning to home, an environment that hadn't exactly been workable for him in the past. As well, this offered me an opportunity to discuss the homeless and what could happen when exposed to the elements (frostbite).

I decided to tell him a story about a doctor who had been exposed to frostbite and subsequently lost the use of his hands and part of his nose. I purposely brought up the tale in order to unearth his feelings about past physical abuse by his biological father. It proved to be a useful anecdote. I explained how the doctor had received reconstructive surgery for his nose and prosthesis for his hands. I am certain that this brought up memories of Brett's laborious operation for reconstructive surgery to his nose when he was abused because he asked me copious questions about the reconstructive surgery to the doctor's nose. Interestingly enough, the doctor's hand prosthesis held no interest for Brett. Instead, he focused on that which was close to his own issue: the injury and subsequent surgery to his nose. Nevertheless, when we returned to the therapy office, he wouldn't touch the feelings that had emerged. His need to approach-avoid the topic was completely understandable. This traumatic experience like any other would need to be metered out in small doses. The following week, I learned that Brett had AWOL'ed (absent without leave) the next day. I was not surprised. The therapy was kicking in and was affecting his psyche. While AWOL'ing can be terribly unsafe for any child, on some levels, for Brett, it turned out to be quite positive. Accompanied by an older boy from another residential cottage, Brett spent the night in a "drug house." While he did not participate in drug-related activities, the experience scared him and he was able to talk about it quite freely with his social worker and anyone who would listen. He seemed very content from that time to reside at Hillside and work towards his discharge plan to return to home.

By the next session, Brett was desperate to see me. I started out by getting three telephone calls from Brett requesting to come early to session. We went for a walk to a corner store to get some snacks and discussed his AWOL experience. On the way, Brett proudly told me about tearing dollar bills in half in order to cheat the proprietor of the store. I told Brett that this was no different than stealing and since he argued the case with me, I invited a response from the storeowner and suggested that we ask him what he thought. The storeowner confirmed that this would be no different than lying or cheating. This seemed to help Brett understand the proprietor's plight when faced with such situations. Because he liked the owner, its meaning generated the capacity for empathy. Brett actually admitted feeling badly about having cheated him in the past.

When we returned from the walk, Brett began to paint the dream sculpture but eventually this became overwhelming for him and we moved on to play with the doll house again. Brett became Brett-noccio and his character began to lie. He would state, "Doctor, Doctor, I hate you, I hate you." He would smile at me as he made this statement and Brett-nocchio's plasticene nose became longer and longer. He invested full throttle in this play: since I had been cast into the role of doctor, I enlisted some other plastic characters as attendees, nurses, and physician assistants. Brett-noccio was rushed to a makeshift hospital and placed on a slab where he received reconstructive surgery to his nose. This allowed me to bring up his nose surgery. Brett said he remembered being in the hospital but *not* the surgery. Brett's ability to relive the scene was concrete enough. At the very last minute, he decided to use plasticene in order to connect the Brett-noccio and Doctor by nose. This act clearly underlined his attachment to me and trust in this process. Alas, our time was up and I reminded him that we needed to end the session. But Brett wasn't ready: he needed to do one more project. Brett picked up a long empty cardboard tube and held it to his nose. Seeing where this needed to go, I decided to extend the session a bit longer. This material was too rich to lose. As doctor, I helped him fashion a nose out of paper towel tubing and then he connected it to his nose and suggested that I connect the opposite end to my nose: I spoke about how important it was for us to stay connected between sessions (metaphorically speaking that is). I gingerly stated, "Only the nose knows, you know." At that point, Brett laughed and again asked if he could have extended time during our sessions and I agreed that I would discuss this option with his teacher. Figure 51 below is a picture of Brett holding his nose. Even the expression on his face bears witness to its deeper meaning.

Of interest was Brett's need to hide the nose under my desk as the session ended. Apparently, it generated enough shame that he didn't want other clients to see it. It is often difficult to give up old habits. Lying can often be a more comfortable place than truth-telling, especially if one is not used to the other's perception except when functioning from this platform. Brett would need time to give up his old semblance, and don a new self-image. Plastic surgery couldn't fix the underlying symptoms or help Brett get used to a more honest self.

In our next session, Brett and I decided to augment "walk therapy" with phototherapy. I had brought in a digital camera to use since Brett was so very adept at using computers. We also had a Polaroid⁂ camera to use for

Figure 51. *Brett-noccio Comes to Life.* Nose at 30 in. long.

instant photography. Brett decided that he wanted to go for a walk at the park across from Hillside and at first we went to the playground area. Considering how much play therapy we had been incorporating in our sessions, it seemed quite fitting. We took turns shooting images of each other and within time, we walked further towards a pond that had frozen over. I took several shots of Brett as he skated on the ice. Brett really enjoyed himself as he danced on the ice. Below is a picture of him in action. For confidentiality, his face (except for his smile) is blackened out. (Since this was taken with the digital camera, it allowed Brett and I to take the image into Photoshop and manipulate the image.) The idea of distorting one's image was quite appealing to Brett, especially since it allowed for reconstructive surgery (if you will) in a different manner. Utilizing the computer for such purposes can be quite freeing. Images can be changed in multifaceted ways and clearly issues can be addressed in a very safe manner. Issues surrounding self-esteem and body imagery can be addressed. Images can be changed, creating great therapeutic potential for the therapist and client. In many ways it can allow both to really look at issues of distortion. Brett really flies on the computer and his ability to use this device as an artistic tool seems to have unlimited potential. As well, his decision as to what to save (as a file) and cast

Figure 52. *Brett on Ice.*

away also has had implication in his treatment.

As we continued on the walk, Brett became excited by a flock of ducks on the ice pond. A toddler and her father were feeding the ducks with small scraps of bread. Brett was quite taken by the sweet idyllic scene. He photographed a beautiful white duck using the Polaroid® and at one point I suggested that if he liked, he could photograph the small child and her father and offer them the photograph as a gift. Brett immediately took to this idea and gave the picture to the father. In exchange and gratitude, the father offered Brett some bread crumbs so that he could feed the ducks. Brett graciously accepted this offer. He fed the ducks a while longer sharing the bounty with me. He photographed me feeding the ducks. Below is his very artistic picture of me feeding the ducks, an interesting metaphor for how he viewed me. His ability to capture images with natural diagonal composition was very interesting to me. In many ways, phototherapy seemed to be a great medium for Brett.

As we prepared to leave, Brett said, "People can be so cool! This is the most beautiful day I have ever had!" I said, "This is only the beginning." And in many ways, Brett's awakening to himself, his issues and his potential, was just that, only the beginning. It is a wonderful rarity when I can truly enjoy the health that I potentiate in another human being and simultaneously myself. This is when primary process gains truly shape the secondary gains in the client. And this is how it should be, an exchange in the process of human healing.

Blurring the Boundaries and the Family Work

Since my return to my studio, my therapeutic interventions have changed considerably. I have been transformed and in the process my work has also

Figure 53. *Therapeutic Feeding.*

Figure 54. *Brett's Ducks.*

transmuted. But this has been a good change. Working with Brett was unlike
any of the work I have done to date, in fact it is some of the most unorthodox clinical work I have yet initiated. My operating outside of the traditional confines of the (therapy) box grew and grew. Through these jaunts, I
learned a lot about Brett: what made him click, what worked, what didn't. I
found out many curious things about Brett as we engaged in rather unconventional practices in the name of "human art." We became art. Everything
we did became an art form. Walks into the woods resulted in constructed
shelters. Ice-skating at a local city park resulted in an opportunity to address
Brett's strengths mutilated by his self-sabotaging behavior. Spring-like days
led to more sublimated activity as we rollerbladed together on the Erie
Canal.

   One day while rollerblading, I remarked about how far we had come from
the studio (in both literal and figurative palettes). Brett's remark was as crystal clear as the azure, cloudless sky above us: "But, this is art. Everything we

do is art." We were becoming art together. This was taking performance art to a new level.

While we still occasionally worked at the studio and many pieces resulted from this individual modality, family therapy became the avenue for some of Brett's most productive treatment. Individually, we were walking a different path. And many began to question my modus operandi. I did not. I did not see this as countertransference, that ugliest of beasts. My colleagues in supervision felt the same way. They saw the changes in Brett both via my documentation immediately following sessions as well as the change and growth in his behavior. I pleaded with the treatment team to consider a less restricted environment. He was ready. But the administrative arm was not. They weren't convinced. They wouldn't let him go.

What happens to a caged animal? Does the creature surrender to authority or store up anger and dwell upon escape? It so reminded me of earlier movies that I had seen about the insane like "King of Hearts" where we become our environments because either we didn't fit in or the community no longer became the desired outcome.

This boy was fighting for his life. And while the social worker left the team and I became the primary and family therapist that held this case together, this multidisciplinary cog, larger than me, offered me little voice nor control in its outcome. It mattered not that I was doing the primary work with the family.

Weeks passed where play and art therapies were combined with ice-skating outside. The traditional space of doing art therapy outside my office allowed me to view Brett in new environs. As a result, self-sabotaging behavior such as purposely hurling himself against the ice-skating wall was addressed. Play sessions followed with Brett forming the Brett-nocchio family of Pleistocene. In one elaborate play session, Brett formed the father shooting a reindeer. This allowed for a lot of aggressive activity and some more discussion about his "nose" and past abuse. Transitioning back to the school and the residential cottage became increasingly difficult. Highly motivated in art therapy, Brett continued to create objects that reflected his need for unconditional nurturance and fear regarding bodily harm. Brett's Pleistocene family members were continually killed off in varied fashion and some members even engaged in suicide. Nevertheless, Brett did not strike me as either homicidal or suicidal: nevertheless, I forewarned staff.

The following week, Brett decided that he needed to make a small fort for his GI Joe⁰ dolls. The fort seemed to be a metaphoric response to his need to be protected, safeguarded and eventually return to home. His urgency in finishing this project was unlike previous projects and highlighted the desperation behind this symbolic container. Moreover, according to Alschuler & Hattwick (1947), his decision to paint the exterior of the box red and the

Figure 55. *Brett's fort for his GI Joe dolls.*

interior black underscored his identification with the environment as aggressive, unsafe and depressing. His addition of the hasp (in order to lock up his valuables) also reflected his concomitant desire to be safeguarded and valued.

Around this time, I began doing co-family art therapy with the social worker. Unfortunately, while the social worker and I operated extremely well together, after the second family art therapy session the social worker informed both the family and me that he would be leaving the case and working in another part of the agency. This was quite a blow for Brett and his family so I decided to continue the family art therapy sessions without a co-therapist until a new social worker was assigned to the case. Primarily, this was due to the fact that the mother truly resonated with me and found the family art therapy approach to be an effective modality.

The Heart of the Matter

Speed up about 35 sessions later. In between this time, there had been eight family sessions and I had conducted all of them with the exception of one co-therapy session with the original social worker assigned to the case. But as explained before, the mother had responded to family art therapy after trying everything from cranial sacraltherapy to medical intervention. She was frustrated by the system and strongly felt that nothing and no one had helped her with her son. That was until me. Janet had voiced on more than one occasion how helpful she felt our work together had been and when I deemed appropriate, I shared some of my psychosocial information, particularly my own struggles as a single parent. I lauded her skills and praised her ability to single-handedly care for her children. Visits to her home were suprisingly refreshing. Her home was immaculate and tastefully decorated. I conducted family art therapy sessions in my office as well as in her home. This kind of interaction really offered a different perspective on the family system. The first time I visited, I brought a loaf of homemade banana bread. The mother reported that after I had left with Brett, his sisters, like hungry wolves, had devoured the bread. I thought it odd that Brett's mother didn't offer up the bread during our meeting, something that I would have done. It dawned on me later that while the house was well cared for that perhaps the cupboards were bare or somewhat sparse in terms of actual food in the house. A month later, when a new social worker came on the scene, I wanted to check out my suspicions and suggested that we do a home visit and cook a meal together as the planned activity. My suspicions turned out to be well-founded.

I knew that on some meta-level, the home visit would offer me a different perspective on the family system while simultaneously providing a nurturing environment during the meeting for Brett's wolf-like, never-full-enough sisters. It also afforded the possibility of role modeling appropriate interactions with Janet's children. The experience was chaotic at best.

In this session, everyone helped prepare enchiladas. The social worker and I spearhead the meal preparation since mother was fairly busy putting out fires with the ever-sulky Samantha. (Samantha was brooding about a neighborhood squabble with one of her friends.) Samantha cried for awhile in the living room and was pretty much ignored by mother until I called her attention to it. Susan, aged seven, was the most industrious family member and practically completed all the work required for production of the meal. But the tenor was confusing at best. Finally, Samantha rather reluctantly agreed to set the table. Once everyone was seated at the table, the social worker turned the discussion toward Brett's last home visit and how he could avoid negative behavior in the future. (It was enough to give anyone indigestion.) But Brett rose above this discussion and suggested ways in which he could temper his volatility including taking "stress walks." It was agreed that mother would begin a trial of taking Brett for day visitation on the weekend as to determine how things went. This was stated after Brett admitted his wrongdoing from the last visit and made it clear that he intended to change his behavior in the future. Everyone left on rather good terms and Brett returned to his residential cottage in good shape.

At this time, I began working with the family system every two weeks. It became clear that the mother was looking forward not only to the sessions but also a place to grieve her own loss issues. It became obvious that Janet needed her own therapy and this was suggested at the next treatment team meeting. It was agreed that the social worker would begin individual art therapy with the mother since my working with her and Billy simultaneously would compromise his individual treatment. Nevertheless, transference issues continued and the mother attached strongly to me. She began to feel that I was the only one that could help her which was one of the reasons why I needed to have another worker in on the case. The stage seemed set for loss and there had been many for this family system: Brett's placement, mother's past abusive relationships, the stress involved in single parenting, animals that had died, social workers that had come and gone, well, the list went on. It seemed natural that the theme of loss had to be openly addressed and resolved before any work could take place.

In the tenth family session, the theme of loss was once against raised. Brett began by making a small man's head from clay while the girls used cookie cutter shapes. In time, Brett began creating a plate of what appeared to be spaghetti (which he later confirmed it was). Mother began making a plaque with four dolphins on it and later described that she often felt "devoured" because she was so overwhelmed with daily living tasks. She also created a log and Brett fashioned a beautiful squirrel and acorn to place atop of it. Prior to Brett's earlier work which was crude and schematic in style, the squirrel and acorn were so well articulated that his work took on qualities similar to what Edith Kramer coined as "formed art." Developmentally, his work had improved and he seemed to be functioning at the Adolescent Stage of Development, age 14-17 years (according to Lowenfeld & Brittain, 1975).

Unlike previous sessions, Samantha did not regress and actually constructed a box, which was later turned into a container for the new cat they were planning to get. Susan made an ashtray for Mom, which allowed me to address her smoking. We talked about her going to see an acupuncturist in order to quit since she had tried absolutely everything. It also allowed me to address how the kids felt about her jeopardizing her health and the fear that they harbored around losing their mother to illness. The pinnacle point of the session was when we were addressing the subject of mother's boyfriend and Brett was able to admit (with my revealing information about my children's response to my dating men) that he was actually both jealous and feared displacement. That was a great turning point. However, had I not brought in my own children's reactions to my dating men, it might have been a long incubation period for such an admission to surface.

Clearly, the objects made, Brett's sea of spaghetti with a floating meatball head suggests his need for unconditional nurturance. Susan's creation of an ashtray captured the essence of loss at its deepest. These were children who clearly had sustained a variety of losses. The fear attached to losing their mother through death was the ultimate statement of abandonment. This resonated with the mother and upon my suggestion, she actually followed through in making an appointment with an acupuncturist that specialized in addictions.

In all there were 59 sessions, (17 of which were family and 8 of which were dyadic group). The remainder was individual sessions. Treatment issues have ranged from forming a therapeutic relationship with Brett to working on feelings of displacement from the family constellation. The individual work revolved around self-expression, self-esteem issues, and the family work engaged in an effort to reconnect Brett with the family members (specifically mother) in an attempt to move towards an eventual discharge to the home. At the time of Brett's last assessment (November of 1997), he was functioning at the low end of the spectrum of the Gang Age Level of Development, age 9 years. Brett seemed cognitively arrested for multiple reasons, which included family of origin issues, low self-esteem, self-abusive behavior, and oppositional defiant behavior.

By spring of 1998, Brett was functioning at the Adolescent Stage of Development, approximately 14-17 years of age. This cognitive jump suggested that Brett was capable of much higher functioning (more suggestive of his intellectual quotient and abilities). Areas of concern were Brett's intermittent and often unpredictable explosive outbursts, seeking attention through self-harming behavior, and continual need for unconditional nurturance. The aforementioned areas coupled with his desire to reconnect to his family of origin were the issues which I addressed both in his individual and family art therapy treatment.

Intervention

Unfortunately, not everyone understands operating outside the parameters of four-walled therapeutic meetings. But Brett and I were beginning to use both phototherapy techniques as well as a digital camera to capture the world around him. Individual sessions would consist of taking walks in the woods and photographing nature as well as each other. The work seemed restorative and productive. When taking Brett out to a local donut shop one day, he began to develop this wonderful relationship with another patron.

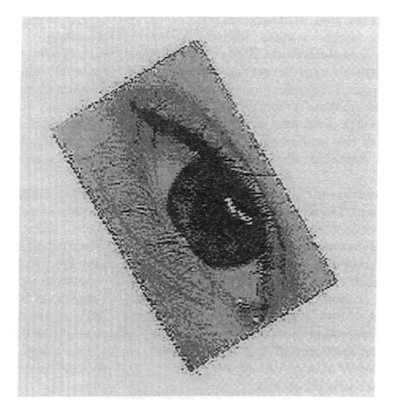

Figure 56. *Manipulated Eye.*

Every Tuesday that we came to the shop, this old woman would be seated opposite us reading her newspaper and eating her donut. Weeks passed by and we listened to her saga of her husband's recent hospitalization and coma state. Brett began photographing her. One day, he approached her with some of the photographs that he had taken of her and many other places. They talked for a full hour and both seemed more fully alive then when they had entered the shop. It was fascinating to see Brett in this altogether different environment. Here, he was polite, appropriate, and downright charming. But when returned to the residence, like an animal about to be caged, he transmuted becoming angry and resistant. To me, it was no surprise but the team was baffled and some were infuriated with me, blaming me for this change in his behavior.

Some proposed that my "unorthodox" methods of treatment bordered on countertransference and many rejected my methodologies. While countless examples of digital work ensued, one of the most unusual alterations was of Brett's eye (figure 56).

Through manipulation with the software, "Image Expert," Brett changed the eye so that it appeared blackened, much like an eye would after being battered. These kinds of images seemed to be somewhat cathartic for Brett but certain members of the team felt otherwise. Instead, they suggested that I had "crossed the boundaries." I insisted that Brett's need, for example, to carry around photos which he had taken of me were merely "transitional objects." Other members didn't think so and insisted that I see him on hospital grounds. I was incensed but wanting the best for Brett; I agreed to drop individual treatment and continue family art therapy.

On the suggestion of the medical director, I continued family art therapy with Brett and his family. Naturally, I had hoped that these interventions would lead to more productive and salubrious treatment for the client and his family. Nevertheless, I worried what effect this would have on Brett. In order to eliminate possible anger regarding this change in Brett's treatment, I informed him that my responsibilities with the agency "had changed" and that was why I wouldn't be seeing him in individual work. At best, this was a white lie. Nevertheless, I knew that for the sake of his treatment, it would be better to handle this delicately.

A few days later, his social worker reported that Brett had expressed suicidal ideation; but in time, things returned to the status quo. It saddened me that the team's ignorance could contribute to such horrific events. While I didn't agree with some of the decisions that had been made, as a team member, I felt forced to comply. Moreover, the team members and I disagreed about Brett's medication. After witnessing this youngster both in and out of the agency and having done a great deal of research on bipolar disorder for my doctoral work, I became convinced that Brett had been misdiagnosed. He was not responding well to his medication of Ritalin[3] and I truly felt that his diagnosis was more reflective of Bipolar Disorder II than ADHD.

According to the DSM IV-R (1997), these were the features that described Bipolar Disorder II personalities:

Diagnostic Features
Bipolar II Disorder: (Recurrent Major Depressive Episodes with Hypomanic Features) The essential feature . . . is a clinical course that is characterized by one or more Major Depressive Episodes . . . accompanied by at least one Hypomanic Episode . . . hypomanic episodes should not be confused with the several days of euthymia that may follow remission of a Major Depressive Episode. (Author's Note: moreover, the presence of a Manic or Mixed Episode precludes the diagnosis of Bipolar II Disorder. As well, as in the previously mentioned diagnosis of Bipolar I Disorder, General Medical conditions and or Schizoaffective Disorders are also ruled out.) The symptoms must cause clinically significant distress or impairment in social, occupational, or other important areas of functioning. In some cases, the Hypomanic episodes do not cause impairment. Instead, the impairment may result from

the Major Depressive Episodes or from a chronic pattern of unpredictable
mood episodes and fluctuating unreliable interpersonal or occupational functioning. . . . (p. 359)

My research on the subject indicated the following information, which I
shared with the mother. (The result was that the psychiatric nurse, while
clearly irate with me since I did not have a degree in psychopharmacology,
reluctantly agreed to a trial of Valproate [commonly known as Depakote].
While I was thrilled, this had personal costs for me which I will detail later.)

Research on Bipolar Disorder and Medication

Bowden and McElroy (1995) looked at the history of Valproate (com-
monly known as Depakote) for the treatment of bipolar disorder. While for-
merly used for anticonvulsive treatment (as early as 1963), its efficacy in
treating bipolar disorder while widely reported had not received FDA
approval for the treatment of bipolar disorder until 1989. Abbott
Laboratories planned a study in hospitalized, acutely manic patients to
address Valproate and its limitations. The question of comparative efficacy
was of particular importance since 30 percent to 50 percent of bipolar
patients did not respond adequately and/or tolerate lithium treatment. In a
study comparing divalproex, lithium and placebo, divalproex or Valproate
was significantly better than placebo as early as the fifth day of treatment and
continued to be so at each rating point in the 3-week trial. (Bowden &
McElroy, 1995, p. 4) The study also established that certain components of
the manic syndrome (elated mood, grandiosity) were more sensitive indicators of response both to divalproex and lithium than were relatively non-specific behaviors, such as agitation.

In another related study by Sharma et al. (1993), Valproate was found to
be effective in the treatment of acute mania, mixed states, and rapid cycling
disorders. The study followed nine patients (with a mean of 50 years old)
who had been previously treated with various psychotropic agents, including
Carbamezapine and lithium. In this study, the effectiveness of lithium coupled with Valproate was being reviewed. It had been purported that the combination of Valproate and lithium transformed lithium non-responders into
responders by causing a shift of the lithium dose-response curve. Patients
omitted from the study were those that had a concomitant disorder of substance abuse, evidence of anti-depressant-drug-induced cycling or mania
during the previous year, or hypothyroidism on the basis of clinical signs and
symptoms such as abnormal thyroid hormone levels.

At the onset of the study, all psychotropic drugs except lithium were elim-
inated. The patients in the study suffered from a rather severe and disabling
form of rapid cycling disorder, the mean duration of which was about 22

years. Eight of the nine patients (six females and three males) showed a marked or moderate improvement on the combination therapy. In three of the patients, (who had not responded to past intervention), there was a dramatic improvement in depressed mood within 24 to 48 hours with the addition of lithium. When the combined therapy was administered, one of these patients was able to leave the hospital after having been hospitalized for six years! Nevertheless, mania relapses were reported in four of the patients when serum levels dropped (Sharma et al, 1993. p. 138).

Results of Medication Changes

It required several weeks for the psychiatric nurse to dispense this medication change but gradually, the mother, the team and I were noticing a change in Brett's functioning both on and off the agency property. After two months of being on this medication, Brett's new social worker with which I had begun doing co-family therapy charted some very significant changes. Brett had remained restraint-free for 30 days. This was an enormous achievement for a boy who averaged 5-6 restraints per week.

This is difficult work that we do. Often what is not understood may be attacked because of its difference and the very nature that this breeds in others. Sameness is greeted favorably because it is the expected norm. But deviation is almost certainly met with indignation and rejection. The day that I was counseled to drop the individual work with Brett, I considered quitting and voiced the same to the chief medical director. I felt that perhaps on some level I had outgrown an agency that left little room for creativity and revolutionary methods of treatment. Naturally, the medical director balked and suggested how much I had to offer the agency via agency-wide training. While I agreed in kind, in spirit, I felt betrayed by the system, which I had served. My decision to continue the family art therapy and drop the individual treatment was a difficult one. But when I searched my heart, I found no wrong in the treatment that I had employed. Instead, I had merely been operating from my heart. I cared about this boy, his outcome, and the success of his transitioning back to his family. It was for those reasons that I had stayed. But I felt squashed by the administrative arm of the hospital.

Sometimes, we do what we have to do. The other alternative would have been to quit, stop educating others as to the work that we do, and ultimately contribute to deleterious thinking. I could not do that because it was Brett that was really at risk here, not me. And oftentimes in these days of CPO's, HMO's, and the Blues, when I looked inside my heart and asked, "Why am I still here?" the answer was abundantly clear: my mission was for the kids. However, sometimes it's just not enough. Several months later, the administration was going through major financial changes. As a result, my job title of 15 years was changed and I was offered a completely different job in the system. I felt overly compromised and decided that it was time to leave the agency. This was a sad and difficult decision for me, especially after 15 years in this agency. But I had witnessed changes that I no longer agreed with ethically and/or medically. As a result, I left. Oddly enough, I had been doing excellent family work with Janet and her boyfriend, Dave. They were not willing to surrender me so quickly.

At a treatment team meeting that I did not attend, the social worker, the mother, the psychologist, and even the psychiatric nurse on the case concurred that had it not been for my treatment and psychotropic intervention, Brett would not be able to be discharged by the summer of 1999. All felt that it was paramount for my services to continue. So in what seemed my last family session, the mother and the social worker asked if I would be willing to continue family art therapy privately. I knew that the mother could not afford my services and clearly, I was invested in this boy's treatment and a successful transition to the home. So what could I do?

I did what any other dedicated practitioner would do. I reduced my rate to a fee that I knew this mother could afford and I agreed to continue family art therapy treatment in the mother's home with whomever most benefited at the time.

Presently, I am testing Susan to determine whether or not she has a learning disability and couples therapy will be continuing with Janet and Dave. In time, family therapy will include all members including mother's significant other, Dave.

I do know that we can only heal others through the healing of ourselves. As Steven K. Levine has said, "If we are not working on our own healing, we certainly can't be contributing to anyone else's healing."

The psychological process of identification has enormous effects on our lives, yet is seldom recognized in ordinary circumstances.

CHARLES T. TART IN *OPEN MIND, DISCRIMINATING MIND*

Chapter 5

DRAGON LORE: A TALE OF COUNTERTRANSFERENCE

Ellen's Story

Ionce knew a deaf baby dragon that held a terrible curse for all that she touched. It mattered not that she was pretty for her fury served to keep all at bay. She never had a mother to teach her dragon lore. Rejected at birth, she had been stolen by a wicked man who rode her body daily and confused the vessel of love. Luckily, she couldn't hear and that protected her from this man's screaming assaults, but it left her unable to speak her truth. Her eyes, too, were weakened from living in dark, dank places. But her deafened ears and broken eyes protected her from witnessing this part that had been so carelessly extinguished. She needed the protection of these and other walls, which she kept between herself and her abuser. When approached, she would thrash out and ravage all with her fiery flames.

I hated working with this dragon baby. She gave new definition to the term "Oppositional Defiant Disorder." You couldn't expect a dragon to do anything in art therapy. She was too busy destroying everything in her path. She'd destroy everything I gave her.

Some days, she would write her name repeatedly on a paper. It mattered not if it fit. She couldn't have cared less. Nothing and everything stimulated her. She would grab anything that was nearby and use it all up, discard it, and then move on to the next kill. Use. Destroy. Discard. Use. Destroy. Discard. All in all the while, her dragon nature grew and grew.

Months passed.

Use. Destroy. Discard. Use. Destroy. Discard.

It took a toll on me. I got so stuck that I just wanted to give her up. I began to take her affronts personally. What needed to happen for both of us was an awakening. She wasn't the only dragon in the room. There was my own sleeping dragon wrapped in a thick fog of countertransference. I was mired in it and it kept me stuck. A fiery dragon raged in her and a sleeping dragon grazed in me. I was blinded by her fire and drugged by my own indifference.

Use. Destroy. Discard. Use. Destroy. Discard.

Always unkempt and unhygienic, the team could never get her to cleanse her fiery ways. But, I began to observe her differently. One day, as she washed her hands at my sink, she drew them to her flaring nostrils and delicately smelled her hands. She liked the smell of the soap. It was really so simple but we all had missed it. Excitedly, I returned her to her residence and asked others if anyone had ever taken her shopping for her own soaps. No one had. The next week, we went to the mall. She bought shampoo, conditioner and body soaps. She showered a lot after that. That baby dragon was encrusted with the grime and dirt of those dank places that she'd had to live in and with the wickedness that had been projected onto her deaf, blind body. Slowly, the crust was washed away and her dragon scales began to fade.

One day, as I laid newspaper on the table for her weekly course of destruction, an advertisement for a little girl "Bake-It-Shop" that was splattered with paint caught her eye. She began to cut it out with a nearby scissors. What was this? The horrible dragon was acting like other 10 year-olds and was interested in typical 10 year-old toys. How had I missed this? We had all missed this. We had only seen the fire-breathing dragon in her, not this.

So we started cooking together like mother and daughter. While we were waiting for the baking, I would slip in a little art. We sewed pillows together, the old fashioned way, by hand.

Just last Monday, this little dragon made an entire meal by herself—flame-broiled, of course. It was amazing to see what happened when this fiery baby used her gifts and controlled her own power.

Now there is a real connection between us but it is one that includes lots of space for both of us and that is the key difference. Wonderful space has opened up. She has gone from overcontrolling to being in control. Like Elinor Ulman once said, she is "making order out of chaos."

Use. Construct. Create. Use. Construct. Create.

To reach her dragon, I had to tame my own in the process. My countertransference dragon has gone back into hibernation. But occasionally, it comes back when I have to let her fail. My own dragon doesn't like failure. But my dragon needs to accept that in failure is the art of learning. I have learned to hush my own dragon that flares up and says "But, but, but …"

We are really cooking now. Most days, she is the chief chef and I am the sous chef. It empowers her and keeps the space between us. Alive and awake, we let our dragons out of the cage so they can co-mingle, create, and burst forth. We are cleansed and healed by our stories and our days ahead.

Use. Construct. Create. Use. Construct. Create.

Performance, Power, and Integrity

The above story about "Scout" was read and performed at the Opening Ceremony of the 29th Annual American Art Therapy Association. It was the result of collaborating with Lynn Kapitan, A.T.R. The story (along with others presented by several other art therapists) was about the dragons with which we have wrestled either professionally and/or personally. But for me, the real power was not in its performance but what it inculcated in me: the opportunity to look at the clinical work and what it instills in me as a practitioner, human being, and artist. This opportunity to write a story with another human being and tweak the work until it was 'just right' was a great gift. But more importantly, Lynn's eye view was wholly different than mine and revealed my "sleeping dragon." In short, this was a great lesson.

Scout's Story

When I write about a client, I search for a pseudonym that helps me relate to that person's personality. The name, "Scout," came to me for a variety of reasons but mostly because the work with Scout has been an adventure for me and, I think, for her. This work impacted not only my modus operandi but also my methodology informed team members and their work with her. While the psychosocial information sometimes seems to be a departure from the story, it necessitates increased understanding of the case. So, I will start with a brief psychosocial picture, the genogram, and an abbreviated art therapy assessment.

Abbreviated Art Therapy Diagnostic Assessment

Name: Scout
BD: 12/18/86
CA: 11.3
Testing Dates: 12/9/97; 12/16/97; 1/12/98; 2/2/98
Test Administered: Cognitive Art Therapy Assessment (CATA) Paint, Clay, and Drawing subtests
Kinetic Family Drawing (KFD)

Reasons for Referral

Scout was referred to me because of her inability to engage in verbal communication. It was thought that she would benefit from the non-verbal approach of art therapy. Additionally, while Scout was deaf, she had not mas-

Scout's Timeline and Genogram

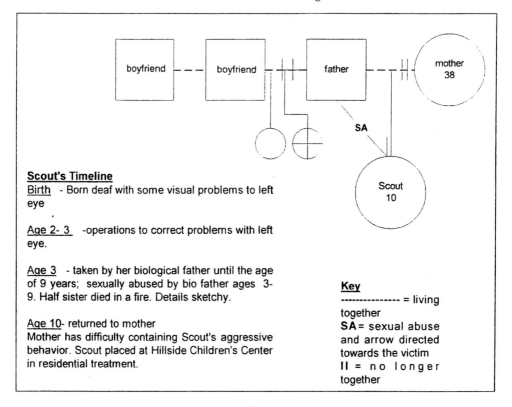

Scout's Timeline
<u>Birth</u> - Born deaf with some visual problems to left eye

<u>Age 2- 3</u> -operations to correct problems with left eye.

<u>Age 3</u> - taken by her biological father until the age of 9 years; sexually abused by bio father ages 3-9. Half sister died in a fire. Details sketchy.

<u>Age 10</u>- returned to mother
Mother has difficulty containing Scout's aggressive behavior. Scout placed at Hillside Children's Center in residential treatment.

Key
--------------- = living together
SA= sexual abuse and arrow directed towards the victim
II = no longer together

tered sign language, couldn't communicate well in either PSE (Pigeon Signed English) nor ASL (American Sign Language) and primarily used gestures and grunting to delineate her needs.

Behavioral Observations

Scout's responses from the very beginning indicated that she had great difficulty with perceptual pathology. Her responses to all the materials, whether clay, painting or drawing media, were extremely uncommon. She approached the materials in a type of staccato fashion: her objectivity towards the materials suggested definite organicity and possible neurological impairment. In fact, I suggested a neurological work-up to ascertain whether or not the perceptual pathology precluded developmental gains. Scout's developmental delays placed her at the Schematic Stage, age 7-9 years, according to Lowenfeld and Brittain. While this delay was not significantly below her age range, her approach to materials indicated severe difficulty with perception. While reports had indicated previous corrective surgery for her lazy-eye syndrome, her visual acuity still seemed inordinately impaired. Given how visually-oriented the deaf population is, it would be devastating if any of her other senses were taxed. In short, if she was experiencing difficulty with perceptual activity, it would be advantageous to take care of those problems before any further deterioration occurred.

Cognitive Art Therapy Assessment (CATA)

Scout chose to work with the clay medium first and decided to make a mirror frame based on one in my office. Interestingly enough, as described above, her approach reflected perceptual pathology and possible visual impairment. While Scout wore corrective eyeglasses and was *not* wearing them at the time, even with corrective lenses, her responses were the same. The way in which she viewed her work when working reminded me of the

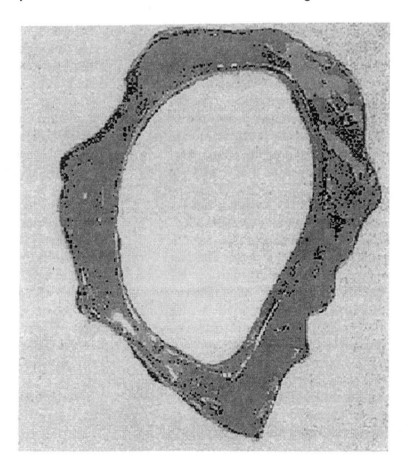

Figure 57. *Scout's Clay Cata Mirror.*

way visually impaired people (who have pinhole or tunnel vision) approach a subject matter: she looked at the material sideways, cocking her head from side to side almost inspecting the material in an attempt to understand it. Also, her approach when working with the materials reflected an unusual internalization process, (e.g., her breathing became heavy as she wedged the clay material) and she appeared to become somewhat exasperated with the actual medium. Nevertheless, her perseverance was quite admirable as she continued to work with the materials. Her method reflected obsessive-compulsive behavior as she repeatedly smoothed the clay until she was pleased with the final product. Her final product, a mirror frame, while created because of one that she had seen in my office, may also have reflected issues surrounding low self-esteem and self-identity conflicts.

Her painting responses reflected similar behavior of obsessive-compulsive activity. Repeatedly, Scout requested pink paper for her paintings. Nevertheless, the color of the paper had always been unrecognizable by the time Scout has finished her project. Predominantly, Scout started off with a meticulous 1/4-inch border completely surrounding the perimeter of the paper. To that she added lines of color and often covered the entire palette with a mixture of purple, red and blue. The choice of colors may have to do with her past history of physical and sexual abuse and concomitant desire to control those feelings surrounding the incident. Almost always, Scout covered this work with a muddy brown color, again reflecting a need to obliterate her feelings. Generally, even before the last layer had dried, Scout would scribe her name as well as the name of her boyfriend onto the surface. She seemed completely unconcerned with the final effect, which resulted in a muddy result.

She refused to do the drawing response of the CATA and again used paints and various media to complete the artwork. In this response, she created a very primitive painting/drawing of a girl with outstretched arms, donning a purple dress and red shoes. The color choice of the clothing and shoes again may have been connected to her previous sexual abuse and her desire to be seductive in fashion. While the arms were outstretched, which suggests Scout's ability to make contact with her environment, the fingers, detailed in mitten-like quality, mirror immaturity. Of interest was the girl's floor length hair, which served to encapsulate and protect the girl in the picture. Again, this may reflect Scout's need for projection from what she probably has perceived as a rather hostile environment.

Developmentally, all three subsections suggested that Scout was functioning at the upper end of the Schematic Stage of Development, age 7–9 years. These results indicated mild developmental delays.

Figure 58. *Scout's CATA Drawing.*

Kinetic Family Drawing Test (KFD)

Scout was quite resistant to drawing her family and did a light pencil drawing of a house, which she described as her mother's house. She placed her mother and her current boyfriend in one bedroom and herself and her boyfriend on the other side. These were the only windows detailed on the house and since they were crafted as second floor windows, clearly the viewer could not witness what was ongoing. Nevertheless, a pathway leading to a large door complete with doorknob invited the viewer. So, while bedroom activities appeared to be cloaked, Scout clearly solicited entry.

Once again, developmentally, Scout's work fell into the same category as before, the upper end of the Schematic Stage of Development, age 7–9 years, according to Lowenfeld and Brittain.

Recommendations and Conclusions

As previously mentioned, Scout clearly seemed to display an inordinate amount of perceptual pathology and possible neurological impairment. Given her propensity for navigating her environment through visual processing of information, a complete neurological work up might turn up more information then currently is on file and is highly recommended. Developmentally, Scout is functioning below age level, although developmentally, she is not terribly off track, approximately the Schematic Stage, age 7-9 years.

While Scout's repertoire includes an obsessive-compulsive behavior while making art projects, this "stick-to-it" quality may actually be strength. She is quite adamant about succeeding in her work and is extremely invested in her artwork, the projects that she makes, and connecting to me.

She has already formed a strong attachment to me (vis-a-vis the testing process) and might actually benefit from sessions that lasted longer than an hour. She always had to be stopped and if she had her way, she would have stayed at the art therapy studio as long as possible. Clearly, if my schedule permitted, I would see her at least twice a week. Unfortunately, given my schedule and her current schedule, treatment precluded more than once a week, individual art therapy. The modality, however, will remain flexible to allow for extended sessions. In time, it would be helpful to enfold the mother, half-sister, and mother's current nuclear family (stepmother, boyfriend, and boyfriend's mother) into family art therapy sessions *if* the plan is for Scout to return to home.

The Countertransference Reign

By the fourth session, I had become increasingly frustrated by Scout's schematic response to the art materials. She seemed totally unconcerned with any materials that I presented to her. I kept reminding myself of Edith Kramer's wise words regarding schema and "allowing for repetitive quality" in the artwork. While I knew that I had to remain patient and accept Scout on her developmental level, I was anxious for movement. The treatment team felt equally impatient. Complaints surfaced from the staff about Scout's unkempt and unhygienic qualities. She hated showering, washing her hair, and performing toiletry necessities. Nothing worked. But one day, as Scout and I washed up from what seemed the 100th repetitive schema painting of obsessive-compulsive three inch lines (and nota bene: this was only the fourth session), I noticed that she was smelling her hands. I asked her if she liked the smell. She did. It dawned on me that this same soap dispenser and soap could be mounted in the bathroom of her cottage residence and perhaps she might be inclined to bathe. I informed the staff. Arrangements were made and Scout began daily showering.

The next week, I suggested a trip to the mall so that we could buy shampoo, conditioner, and soaps that appealed to her. In a week, she had plowed through all of it. In short order, we realized that we needed to ration her supplies. Her response to the toiletries was no different than her reaction to the art materials: like a hungry baby, she devoured everything in her path. This was Scout: Use. Destroy. Discard. She responded to all materials in the same way that her biological father had treated her, as an object to be used, destroyed, and discarded.

She knew no other way. And every time I witnessed this reaction to the materials, my countertransference went through the roof. I can't say for certain why this bothered me so much. It reminded me of Edith Kramer's reaction to young Martin in her famous text, *Art as Therapy with Children* (1975). In this marvelous story, Martin abused the art materials causing Edith to push him up against the wall. His response, "You make my dick itch" was something I recalled from my days as a graduate student while under her tutelage. That brave admission had always stuck in my mind perhaps as a constant reminder of our human fallibility.

While I had not yet shoved Scout up against the wall, every particle of me wanted to. A few weeks later, unabashed, I admitted my frustration during a treatment conference. I announced my desire to surrender the case. The social worker implored me to try another month. Reluctantly, I agreed.

As usual, I had been missing all her cues because of my own agenda. Weeks passed by. Scout would enter the office and ask to make hot chocolate or tea. It became almost ritualistic. She would spend 30 minutes in the process, mesmerized by my hot water machine. There was never enough time to make art, only drinks. Occasionally, she would use my cassette recorder, don earphones, crank up the volume so loud that it hurt my ears, and pretend to hear music. While I checked the possibility of any decibel intake, occasionally she could feel the beat of the music but often she could not discriminate between static, conversation, or music. It saddened me to watch her so desperately attempt to fit into the hearing world as she continued to reject both her language and deaf culture.

One day, she picked up my telephone and pretended to call her mother. It reminded me of E.T. phoning home. She spent the next 50 minutes using both of my telephones and pretending to have a hearing conversation. Scout was unwilling to work on any artwork and this time after making herself some tea, she would repeat phrases like, "Mama, I love you. I miss you." Overall, she used this continually as a defense and avoided interactions with me. At one point, I asked her if she remembered trying to call her mother from her father's house (allegedly trying to conjure up the sexual abuse issues) and she said, "Yes." While I attempted to engage her further regarding this admission, she shut down. She appeared sullen, dejected, transfixed.

I decided to focus on her need to connect with her mother. This continual phoning home reminded me of dialing "911." While Scout was able to use a TDD (telecommunication device for the deaf) and had access to one both in my office as well as in her cottage residence, this phoning was of a very different order. So I suggested that we try a more realistic method of contacting her mother.

My attempt to enlist her in any art activity failed so as she repeatedly conversed with no one on the phone, I ended up making a card for her to send to her mother that stated how much Scout missed and loved her. She took it back to the cottage to be mailed. But I still had missed what was going on.

I don't know what I was thinking but, I suggested that perhaps she didn't want to be in art therapy any more and perhaps her time would be better spent doing other things. I suggested giving her time to someone whom might actually want to be here. She didn't seem to care one way or the other. My countertransference had hit an all time high. I was totally stone-blind to the work we were doing. I had to remove my shrouded visor to see that we were actually doing art, albeit without art materials.

Then an awful thing happened. One day, while Scout was at the school connected to the program, she succeeded in seducing an older, deaf boy. They were unescorted as they walked from one building to another. How this occurred was being investigated but the damage had been done. Scout had been forced sexually by the older resident. While she had initiated the venture, the deaf boy involved had been charged because she was a minor and he was quickly discharged to another program. Meanwhile, Scout's mother, Ellen, flew in from New York City and stayed for two weeks until all of her questions had been answered. This created a golden opportunity for me. The mother, who clearly was bipolar disorder and in a manic phase due to the current events, was trying everyone's patience, except mine. (Maybe it was because of the bipolar component with which I so identified in my own family of origin issues, maybe it was the fact that my office was in another building from the residence and I hadn't been "living" with this mother hanging around, or maybe I just liked her as a person. But whatever it was, I decided that Ellen was there and desperately was needing as much therapy as her child and I decided to offer her an hour of family art therapy in my office.) She thought it was a novel idea and came to my office with Scout. We also had talked about the idea of trying to talk to Scout about the rape; up until that point, Scout refused to talk with anyone about the situation (including a well-meaning police officer sans interpreter.) Hey, it was a crapshoot, but it worked.

I suggested using clay for all the obvious reasons. She and Scout made a heart together from clay. While working with the materials, Ellen repeatedly admitted to her anxiety around Scout and feeling like she was "walking on eggshells." I acted as interpreter for Scout transliterating for both the mother and Scout. Ellen talked painfully about giving up her children to be raised by others as well as the kidnapping of Scout by the father. Scout just watched, stroking the heart-shaped clay as I signed mother's story. Occasionally, she watched my signing and then other times, she focused on the clay artwork. Exactly how much she paid attention to will never be known but after Ellen had admitted her deepest fears and regrets, followed by, "Boy, are you lucky to have such a great job!" I decided that perhaps I ought to enlist Ellen to co-lead the session. In other words, I empowered her both through my language and guidance to broach this very painful topic with Scout. Ellen was able to extract information about Scout's sexual activity (rape) with the other client. In Scout's limited, personalized language system she admitted that the boy "didn't force (her)" but clearly stated that she didn't want to have sex. I encouraged Ellen to talk about the incident quite graphically and then Scout admitted that the boy had ripped her vagina during penetration. Tears were shed as Scout confessed both her physical and emotional hurt and the scene practically moved me to tears.

After that, during the next week of team meetings, I aligned with the mother and offered her support and encouragement needed to investigate the situation. I also defended her insistence that a "plan" be instituted in order to safeguard future clients from such an experience. It was a wonderful opportunity for not only me but also the team to rally and support this woman. Then, Ellen returned to the city and took Scout there for a week. When Scout returned, she appeared transformed. Her hair had been dyed and cut and she arrived in preteen, inappropriate clothing. You see, Ellen, a former prostitute, really lacked the basic skills in mothering. But, in family work you need to look for the strengths and work with what you can.

Shortly thereafter, Scout harbored this fantasy that she was pregnant. Naturally, with the mother's permission, we had safeguarded against this. But still, Scout was obsessed with the idea. This presented an opportunity for me to focus on sexual education and issues surrounding abuse and love. Connecting this to her father's abuse was a more difficult task, which Scout steadfastly avoided. So finally seeing the light, I decided to go with whatever Scout presented. I finally got it. I knew that she would talk about issues when she could and no matter how much I prodded, it mattered not. Scout was on her own time, not mine.

A Turning Point

Fourteen sessions into treatment: anybody else would have perceived our work successful but I was still frustrated. Scout was defensive as usual to start; she didn't want to work on a pillow project which we had started. Disgusted, I took up the work and threaded the needle. After watching me work, she reluctantly stitched a little. Then she disbanded the project after cutting out pictures from a magazine of dress-up clothing for girls, nail polish, and age-appropriate toys. Most of the things she cut out had to do with food (nurturance issues) or play items such as a "Bake-It-Shop." I suggested that perhaps we cook together next time. Eureka! She loved the idea! After all this time, my blindfold finally fell away. I was able to see what she had been craving, a mother-daughter experience that was not only age-appropriate but also laced with corrective experiences. The very last 15 minutes of session, Scout worked very closely with me, touching my hand to her hand, as she stitched the pillow together. It was the first time she had initiated physical contact.

The following week, I arrived with food for us to bake and the pillow. She was incredibly independent and stubborn all at the same time and I realized it would take an enormous amount of work to assist her with the cooking while not maligning our relationship. I had to suck in my defenses, which leapt before me like some old wound. My need to control was full throttle; I had to allow for mistakes, hers and mine. This was not easy since I deal in black and white and rather painfully avoid the grays. It has taken me a long time to become more tolerant as a human being. But this case and many others have helped.

I stepped outside myself and let her make mistakes as well as discover answers. In time, I enlisted the help from the nutritionist at work and we went beyond making eggs and desserts to creating an entire meal for the cottage. Scout was so proud and so was I. But one day, while waiting for something to come out of the oven, we were sewing a pillow together in the adjacent room. She listened and watched my instruction and then took up the threaded needle and while I held the material in place she sewed the edges closed. She remarked at two rings that I always wear on my hands, my father's ring and my mother's engagement ring. She asked about them and wondered who gave them to me. I decided to tell her the truth behind why I always wear these rings. I don't know why but it just fell out as naturally as it would at a coffee klatch with another human being. I told her that since my father and mother had died, I always wore these rings to remind me of them. (I have always referred to the accident that took my father's life as the "day my parents died" because while my mother survived, she was *not* the same woman.) She paused, looked deeply into my eyes and told me about the time her half sibling died and how she had always felt somewhat responsible for the death. For the first time, we were able to process the grief she felt around loss of her family. The work had finally begun.

These days, Scout and I continue to work on corrective mother-daughter experiences. There are times when I still get frustrated as we move two steps forward and then two steps backward. But we are in this work together, and like life, the work ahead needs to be paced according to what one can handle. I no longer push for the jugular with Scout. We continue to make food together, create art projects, and sew our histories together from the tattered threads that we have to offer each other as people. Two human beings really cooking. This is Art.

Figure 59. *Scout Cooking.*

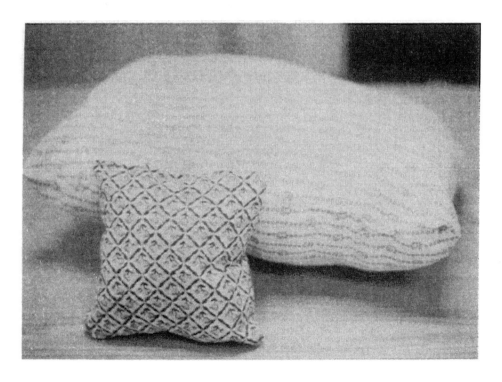

Figure 60. *Scout's Pillow.*

What are we trying to make sense of? What sense can come from a stroke of a paintbrush? This is the game, and I just continue to draw and paint and write hardly ever knowing why. I just know that if I don't, the line from the sane to the insane grows smaller, and at the end of the line I hope someone else will understand how I feel.

LORI WUEST, 1999, UNPUBLISHED MASTER'S THESIS, FROM THE NAZARETH COLLEGE ART THERAPY PROGRAM, CREATIVITY AND EPILEPSY: A CLINICAL AND EXPERIMENTAL EXPLORATION

Chapter 6

COGNITION, THOUGHT PROCESSES, AND LANGUAGE SYSTEMS: INTERVIEWS WITH OTHER ARTISTS

In this chapter, I will explore the links between madness, creativity, and the continual quest for transformation via other thinkers as well as through my own experiences as an artist/writer and human being. What intrigues me is the creative process, how it surges in all of us and exactly where the similarities lie between other artists/therapists and writers and myself. So I decided to canvas a few in my field as well as creative artist/writers from other fields. The interviews summarized the following areas, which I had been investigating:

1. How writing informed each artist's creativity or how one's creativity informed one's writing.
2. Inspect the interplay between the art medium and the writing.
3. Examine the differences between artist/writers when they are employed in the writing mode versus another creative mode (e.g., art, poetry, music, dance, performance, or the like).
4. Question the dissociative properties of engaging in the creative act (that is what occurs if one splits off from oneself in order to engage in the creative process).
5. And lastly, asking artist/writers to describe what happens when engaged in the state of *elemental play* or continuous flow.

I questioned a variety of people and frankly I could have just interviewed people and written a book in itself. But I wasn't attempting to gather data for the purpose of either quantitative or qualitative analysis. Instead, it was more a journey of comparing notes: asking fellow artists how this dualistic, artistic nature both affected them and/or influenced them in their work and creativity. Truly, I was trying to ascertain whether or not others grappled with the same issues that I did. For me, this dualistic nature of mine hasn't exactly co-existed smoothly. These twin-like cells, sloughing off on each other, have often caused undue duress in me as an artist/writer. Sometimes they seemed to be unnecessarily at war with one another.

People that I interviewed were mostly other art therapists that I knew and respected as both artists/writers. But I also spoke with other writers that vacillated between investigative reporting and poetry or fiction writing and music. The opportunity to speak to people about these sacred aspects of creativity was a great privilege. It often affirmed and reinforced my feeling of not "being the only one" who struggled with these issues: that was a comfort in and of itself.

Levinthal (1988) suggested that we have been ineptly named *Homo Sapiens* and should instead be called *Homo Ludens* (or the one who plays). He proposed that creativity be at the core of transcendence. Other theorists such as Csikszentmihalyi have presented invoking creativity in order to propel humankind   towards   an   evolutionary   pathway.   According   to Csikszentmihalyi (1996):

> Of all human activities, creativity comes closest to providing the fulfillment we all hope to get in our lives. Call it full-blast living . . . The excitement of the artist at the easel or the scientist in the lab comes close to the ideal fulfillment we all hope to get from life, and so rarely do. Perhaps only sex, sports, music, and religious ecstasy—even when these experiences remain fleeting and leave no trace—provide a profound sense of being part of an entity greater than ourselves. (P. 34)

Csikszentmihalyi goes on to add (parenthetics mine):

> If I had to express in one word what makes their (creative individuals) personalities different from others, its complexity. They show tendencies of thought and action that in most people are segregated. They contain contradictory extremes; instead of being an "individual," each of them is a "multitude." (p. 34)

While the divided self often subdivides into areas that one might determine to be madness, it is important to look at exactly where the line must be drawn between creativity and madness, that is if one can draw one at all. In a written correspondence to Ai Gvdhi Waya, (otherwise known as Dr. Eileen Nauman), who authored *Soul Extraction and Recovery*, she delineated this positioning quite clearly to me. She wrote:

> Creativity and madness are one in the same, didn't you know that? It is HOW we integrate it (or not) that is the real question. Is it seamless, and therefore, part of us every living, breathing moment (as it is in my case) or is there a division, a chasm, through which the artist must 'switch' to connect to it? (either through drugs, alcohol or some other hallucinogenic route)??? (Personal Communication, 1997)

Naturally, I felt compelled to explore those very points raised by Ai Gvdhi Waya and thus this brought me to creativity, madness, and depression.

In a special issue devoted to the subject of creativity, *Discover* (1996) compiled several articles on this much-watched subject. Given the amount of research I had recently surveyed linking manic depression and creativity, I was not surprised to read the following statement: "Great artists are more likely to suffer from manic depression than the rest of us. So claims the latest in a long line of explanations that link mental illness with genius" (Gutin, 1996, p.75).

The eminent psychologist, Kay Redfield Jamison, who has been touted as the defacto person for the present day art-and-madness link compiled an extensive list of musical, visual, and literal artists that read like an "A-list for the cocktail party of the millennium" (Gutin, 1996, p.77). Naturally, this raised quite a few eyebrows since many skeptics doubted the validity of assigning diagnoses such as manic-depression retroactively to dead artists. Devil advocates such as psychiatrist Frank Johnson of the University of California at San Francisco pointed out that in the 1960s, alcoholism was the "literary disease of choice" and still earlier in the century epilepsy and syphilitic paresis were linked to genius. In fact, the profile of Vincent van Gogh and his diagnosis caused divisive questioning in the etiology of his madness. Much has been written about van Gogh's periods during his asylum stays that ranged from December 1888 through May 1890 and many interesting hypotheses have been suggested. I believe Meissner (1994) best summarized van Gogh's state in the following paragraph:

> . . . the leading candidates in the differential diagnosis have been paranoid schizophrenia, manic depression, alcoholism, syphilis, and epilepsy... The possibility of an affective disorder is supported by Vincent's recurrent depression and possible manic periods. . . . If we add into this already overburdened situation the possibility of his having contracted syphilis, considering the ravages of tertiary syphilis, particularly the possibility of general paresis, we have a highly complex and difficult diagnostic picture that we could never hope to unravel at the removal of a century. (p. 300)

In short, they remained clueless. For as Jamison's critics have pointed out, it is truly impossible to accurately diagnose a person's disease when past diagnostic measures were not only crude and furthermore imprecise but also records were sketchy at best.

The artist, van Gogh, wrote the following account while institutionalized in an asylum, a place where he admittedly felt safe from his madness and the world (Meissner, 1994):

> Work distracts me infinitely better than anything else, and if I could once really throw myself into it with all my energy, possibly that would be the best remedy. . . . I feel like a fool going and asking doctors permission to make pictures. Besides, it is hoped that if sooner or later I get a certain amount better, it will be because I have recovered through working, for it is a thing which strengthens the will and consequently leaves these mental weaknesses less hold.
>
> (Letter 602)

Intriguing to me was that van Gogh knew intrinsically how to heal himself but he had to *convince* his doctors of his plan. And still in contrast to that error, van Gogh *knew* how to operate in wellness. Today, these same ministries are detailed quite specifically by Myss (1996) who insists that we have the potential to "heal ourselves." Myss concurred with the writings of Becker (1985) (who experimented with NEJ's -neuroepidermal junction) and talked about neuropeptides (the chemicals triggered by emotions) housing emotional information in our cells which then translated that data into matter. Tuning into our intuition and directing that "energy" in positive fashion was what Myss detailed as the directive toward entreaty and health. Myss (1996) very clearly detailed the steps to take to intuit spirit and health into our anatomy and mentioned several principles for creating such ministry.

An abundant amount of sense is her basic premise of "biography as biology": "As our lives unfold, our biological health becomes a living breathing biographical statement that conveys our strengths, weaknesses, hopes, and fears" (Myss, 1996, p. 40).

So the debate remains: is creative genius synonymous with mental illness? To generalize and say affirmatively that it *is* would be a mistake but merely dismissing this notion seems equally simplistic. It is quite possible that there exists a mixture of both realms thus giving way to the theoretical underpinnings of Jamison.

I consider myself a highly creative individual. Having grown up with a manic depressive mother, I can honestly say that I feared being like my mother all of my life, ran from the idea for years, and have discovered much to the mutual satisfaction of both my therapist and myself, that while I have much in common with my mother, *My Mother, My Self* can earnestly be reserved for the ranting of Nancy Friday.

One thing is sure, dis-ease has survived a vigorous history of being responsible for the often unfathomable in personality and behavior. Maybe Susan Sontag was right when she mused in her landmark book, *Illness as Metaphor*, that insanity is "merely the current vehicle of our secular myth of self-transcendence."

The Interviews

While not the first person that I interviewed, **Parker J. Palmer**, well-known author, educator and proponent of spiritual inquiry radically changed my thinking about this dualistic process. In the interview, Parker connected his own plunge into depression and its impact on his work. Parker is extremely well-known for his non-fiction voice in such hallmark books such as *The Active Life, The Company of Stranger: Christians and the Renewal of America's Public Life, The Promise of Paradox: A Celebration of Contradictions in the Christian Life,* and *To Know As We Are Known: A Spirituality of Education.* Nevertheless, what Parker most identifies with is his true love, poetry.

Here are some excerpts from the interview:

Interview With Parker J. Palmer

E: How do you view yourself as a writer/artist?

P: I think of different inner experience when working on prose as contrasted when working on poetry–prose is much more of a labor and a very intentional kind . . . Sit down and do it. Poetry gets done to me rather than me towards it. It feels like a false distinction–the poetry is more spontaneous: (it) tends to erupt–you get a line that won't leave you alone . . . and you see where it takes you. With prose, you try and make your case and make it as cogent as possible and as compelling as possible. If you push that further, you allow it to be poetic, to not overstructure it, to save its spontaneity, to accept the fact that even though it feels like you need to make a linear argument on the page, you allow it be more circular rather than a forced march from point A to point B. How do I protect the spontaneity where the prose is more organic than manufactured? With the poetry, once you have the inspiration, you need craft and you need hard work but a different course.

E: When you write, you actually craft it?

P: Yes, I do. It's odd. That dominant image is given and it's non-negotiable and the rest of the poem has a lot of negotiation in it. You lay down a line and it doesn't ring true and if you're running in a poetic form like sonnets, there you have to be aware of a lot of things, meter and beat, etc. Part of every artist's experience is not ultimately constraining but strangely liberating. Talk about returning to scenes (for example) to help crystallize the scene so that it becomes indelible.

E: So it becomes more like a canvas?

P: Yes, that surface distinction between the labor and the inspiration is ultimately false because both types need labor and inspiration. One thing that helps is to look at the end of the process (I'm about to publish my 7th book) and its like a baby (labor of love) but inwardly, I am more thrilled to see a poem in print than to have a book in my hands from a mainstream publisher. I am wrestling with what is the difference between them … there is something precious about a poem–there is a lot of myself in my books but a poem puts you out there much more focused and crystallized in a microcosmic way.

E: Yes, I know what you mean, it's like taking a walk in the words and seeing a leaf and then all of a sudden, bang, it's right there.

P: A book though is much more multilayered, complex.

E: A friend of mine said that Poetry is the Language of the Psyche.

P: Yes, the language of the Soul . . . but when you have an extended case to
make (such as in a book) it's different, whereas a poem is like bang—here is
an example: I have written about my experience with clinical depression and
my struggle through to the other side. I have a poem that was written out of
that experience. This was written in the middle of depression as I was walking down a country road past a plowed field:

Harrowing

> The Plow has savaged this sweet field
> misshapen clods of earth kicked up.
> Rocks and twisted roots exposed to view
> last year's growth demolished by the blade
> I have plowed my life this way,
> turned over a whole history,
> looking for the roots of what went wrong,
> until my face is ravaged, furrowed, scarred.
> Enough.
>
> The job is done.
> Whatever has been uprooted, let it be.
> Seedbed for the growing that's to come.
> I plowed to unearth last year's reasons.
> The farmer plows to plant the greening season.

It wasn't that all the introspection, analysis was wasted, it's that whatever has
been uprooted, let it be. This essay about this will make this more accessible
to other people. The essay is more opaque because every line I write takes
me farther and farther away from the immediacy of the experience. It's
almost a distortion of the experience but the poem grabs it and takes me
right back to that day walking right next to that field and to that energy that
said, it's not that the plowing was wrong but that you misunderstood the why
of it.

E: When you write your poems, you are in a very different state then as a
prose writer: can you describe what the difference is if it's possible and what

that feels like. I talk about how writing non-fiction is outcome-based but with a poem you are moving in a very small, compartmentalized area so you can't go off and I am wondering how that feels for you intrinsically.

P: Stimulates a whole lot of thoughts. I have been most open writing when I am in some kind of crisis–I am madly in love or in the pits of Hell. A poem is some way of taking a spinning energy field and crystallizing the heart of it.

E: Do you divide off when you do that? Do you sort of separate?

P: Maybe there is a paradox. You separate in a way that brings you more deeply into yourself.

E: That's what I meant.

P: Yeah. That would fit with my experience. The poetry is very much about the self. Now when I write prose, it's coming from me. I have this very deep commitment that the writer should do the work rather than the reader. I feel as a writer that I need to anticipate the questions that a reader has and answer them. So the topic has to be delivered with clarity and in a way that really communicates. With a poem, I don't feel that obligation.

E: That is so interesting; but you don't feel that way with a poem because you are hoping that they'll question?

P: Yeah, I am hoping they will question with a book, too, but I don't want their question to be based on the fact that I did a sloppy job putting it together. With a poem, like *Harrowing*, there are such rich meanings, but *Harrowing* is how life gets and I don't know if the reader is going to pick up both meanings of the title and I don't care. It's an image that sits out there and it's in my heart and someone else's heart and they do what they do with it.

E: Yes, I know what you mean and I also don't really care if the viewer/ reader gets it or not.

P: Exactly. But with an extended thesis, I feel the need to explain myself. If I am telling the story, you just tell the story. Jesus said it best when they asked him, "Why do you keep telling stories?" Jesus said, "So those that are capable of getting it, will get it, and those who won't, won't." And yet there is a different discipline in the two forms.

E: Can you talk about where you go when you divide off? I talk about it as "*elemental play*" in my book, when I am in a creative immersed state, I split off from myself to go off to what I consider a healthier dissociative part of myself. Is that sort of what you are talking about when you go in deeper?

P: Very interesting question in the way you are framing it. There is sort of an ego self–how I want others to receive me, how I am projecting myself, and with that I am always manipulating and worrying and trying to get things to come out my way. Then there is what Thomas Merton called the "True Self" . . . the kind of self that doesn't depend on being effective, doesn't lust for praise, doesn't live in fear of blame, but just is. The movement that I am talking about takes me from ego-self to true self.

E: Would you call that id?

P: Yes, the primitive place–you have full access to your own Eros, sexuality with other beings. That is absolutely true.

E: When I am in this state, eight hours can pass and its because I am in this other state of being. It's that state that I am talking about returning to.

P: For me, it's another place. It's a place of deep stillness. For me, the id is an energetic place. But there is some kind of still center that's full of life and yet absolutely quiet. There isn't any swirling energy, it's probably the most primitive state of all, and it's like pure being. It's a state I reach sometimes through Quaker meeting or sitting in silence. It's the center that Taoists have written about where the center which you can watch yes and no chasing each other. It's also the moment before creation.

E: That is an interesting way to look at it: the moment before creation: it's that ah-ha place. . . . Don Jones, the founding father of Art Therapy, has called it "aesthetic arrest."

P: Creation could be my writing a poem or your creation of a canvas or the moment before the Big Bang cosmologically speaking or the moment before God said, "Let there be light." Nothing exists and yet the possibility for everything exists.

E: I think that getting back to that state (our roots), I think that when you get there that this state informs all thought processes, all cognition for human beings.

P: Absolutely, I believe that completely. It's a place where you can revision yourself and your possibilities and nothing exists but the possibility for everything exists or anything exists. In *Harrowing*, the poem takes me to that place. . . . I take a deep breath and I behold the possibilities for my life: I don't have to be a depressed person anymore, I don't have to wear this mask, whatever it is. I can take a new step in another direction. And then as soon as I take that step, as soon as you put a word on the page or a daub of paint on the canvas, then consciousness returns. And the possibilities start narrowing down because you've chosen this word instead of that word or you have chosen brown instead of blue, and immediately, you have a trajectory of some sort. And the possibilities close down further and further and finally you have this book or that painting out of all the gazillions of possibilities that existed earlier.

E: So that's why you call it that point just before creation?

P: Yes.

E: That's interesting. That is what I consider the state of elemental play. But Levinthal talked about the state of Homo Ludens . . . before the light bulb goes off. Maybe it knows when you are done.

P: And when you lay that line down or the scientist decides to pursue that hypothesis or that (which immediately eliminates particular data) there is energy and life in that because life is about making those choices and making those commitments. There is life that comes out of that trajectory.

This was an amazing conversation for me. It stimulated all kinds of thoughts and concretized that we were operating along similar pathways. Many other writers also reaffirmed this for me. But when Parker talked about that "energy and life" which formed that pathway towards choice and commitment, I immediately thought of Ai Gvdhi Waya, author, shaman, and expert on homeopathic medicine.

Ai Gvdhi Waya, otherwise known as Dr. Eileen Nauman, author of several texts including the heralded, *Poisons that Heal*, and author of over 50 fiction works (published under the pseudonym of Lindsay McKenna) had very distinct views on this creative process, again many akin to my own:

Interview with Ai Gvdhi Waya

E: Mainly, I know you are a shaman and that your specific area is homeopathic medicine but I am just curious as to whether you see yourself as well as an artist? Because although I don't know much about your personal background, I would guess that you have a lot of artistic background as well? Is that correct or incorrect?

A: That is correct but then again everything is creativity. Whether you are doing homeopathic case taking, granted there is always a structure in the foundation that is left brain to it. But the artistic interpret art part of it is right brain and it is always present, no matter what you do. I don't care what it is.

E: I guess that is the reason, I didn't really know that about you per say, I just felt it from reading your book and that was one of the reasons I wanted to interview you, because... I guess what I am investigating at this point, is how art, whether it is writing homeopathic medicine, or doing medical intuiting, or what ever it is that you consider your art form, informs your writing your cognition basically all of you. I have been interviewing a whole bunch of different writers, who are also artists, and I am curious about how the art informs you specifically.

A: I sort of need to tell you what goes on in me in my creative process, in my writing. I can sit down and literally in 2 1/2 hours write 20 to 30 pages. From 9 in the morning to 11:30 in the morning, do not bother me. I turn off the phone, I am left alone and I am not disturbed, because if somebody walks in it breaks that connection and it really jumps the Hell out of me and it makes me really angry and irritable for starters. Very basically, if I want to sit down and write, I feel the shift and it is a very obvious shift in my consciousness and I see a huge frame and it is like watching a color movie and I see all the players in the scene and I see what they look like and what they are wearing and where they are. Basically I put myself inside their bodies to see how they are feeling and then I basically see myself as a scribe, translating and writing down what is going on.

E: That is really fascinating that you said that because a friend of mine, Bruce Moon, recently wrote that he considered himself no more than an "imageorator." Is that sort of how you see yourself, because you say that you put yourself inside people's bodies and that you become scribe-like, so you become the orator of their imagery?

A: Yes, that is very true but while I am inside that body I am feeling everything that person is feeling, sometimes it is a whole lot of fun but sometimes it is not. Sometimes it is extremely painful . . . What I do as a shaman and what I do as a writer, there are similarities between the two but are very different. When I am working shamanistically with a person, I am running that person's crap through my body, getting rid of it. When you are writing, let's say a book, I do not have to get rid of anything.

While the rest of the interview zigzagged into Ai's experience as a Native American shaman, something Ai mentioned struck me. While writing is not necessarily the same as shamanistic work, whereby you take on another person's pain and rid them of the emotional and physical blocks, in many ways, I think that the process is similar, at least for me. If I **don't** rid myself of that energy, then I am poisoned by it. For me, the need to temper that creative outpouring is identical. In this, I closely identify with Vincent van Gogh's earlier statement that work distracted him better than anything else, and in fact perceived it as a medicinal remedy. Perhaps this is what **Shaun McNiff, Ph.D, H.L.M, A.T.R, B.C.**, author, artist, and art therapist truly meant when he talked about dialoguing with the image in his text, *Art As Medicine*.

Interview with Shaun McNiff

E: Can you tell me how you view yourself as a writer as opposed to an artist? Is there any difference? Do you really see it as all the same thing?

S: When people say to me, "What do you do?," it's like, oh My God, one of those impossible existential questions. I do tend to accept the definition of an artist. I really wouldn't call myself a writer even though I have written all these books. Maybe D.H. Lawrence might see himself as the same way, as an artist.

The only reason I write books is because of what I have done with the arts. This springs from what I did in the first years of art therapy. I found that I had to get that message out. Then I found writing became a part of my life. A lot of the writing is literary non-fiction. It is not just academic writing. But it all comes from having a message, having something to say about creative arts therapy. It is not because I set out to be a writer.

In terms of responsive artmaking (as Bruce talks about) (Author's Note: Shaun is referring to Bruce Moon and his 1996 text here), I have found with my own work and other people, storytelling is a way to respond to the image. What I am constantly doing is responding to art with art, visual art work with story, writing, movement, sound, and performance. Why? Because I find that it keeps moving the energy. It responds to art with art. It doesn't shut it off. I find that analytic explaining of a picture shuts it off. I describe it as "defending against the image" and, you know, the "label." I give a sequential narrative about how I created the picture but I find that very limiting. In terms of my experience with depth psychology the narrative is much more limiting than a much more imaginative way of responding to the image with art.

I have thought about this for years. . . . The conclusion that I keep coming to is that I don't think that there are any direct influences from one to another. My creative process really requires varied outfits. I have to do more than one thing. I can't just paint. In order to be a creative person, I have a need to write things, paint, and work with people. When I look at my adult creative life, those things have balanced out and been pretty consistent for the last 30 years.

E: Is there an interplay for you—going from your painting to your writing, or is it a very separate act? Do they mesh somehow? Does one feed off of the other?

S: Sometimes. For me, I don't think so much in terms of literal connections from one thing to the other. I just have to do the different things. For me it is an energetic connection. If I am writing something and continue it into a painting . . . John Paul Richter talked about the creative process in the 1800s in the book *School for the Aesthetics* that he wrote. In order for the imagination to bloom, it requires all the faculties. I have always found this to be the case— exercising my creativity, thoughts, energy, that somehow or other I have always had to be involved in more than one thing. I have always used all of the arts. In terms of what are the motivational links? I don't know. Who knows? It is an energetic thing. It's putting them all into the cooking pot and they take endless combinations.

E: Do you ever divide off when you write in a healthy dissociative manner?

S: I get into a trance but I don't disconnect. What I do is concentrate on what I am doing. My family is always amazed at how I can listen to music and go back into it (writing) . . . now it is like second nature. I shift from one thing to another. I have incredible powers of concentration. I have learned how to shift from this thing to that thing and make good use of my time.

E: That shifting is a creative process in itself.

S: Yes, it permeates everything I do, learning how to be present.

E: So, could you describe when you are actually in the state of creation? That is what that feels like, that state of flow which I call *elemental play* in the book?

S: To me it's all about building. I write about it in this last book, *Trust the Process.* It is all about letting go. I remember as a child being stuck because I was always trying to think too much about what it is I was trying to do. What I have learned to do over the years, whether it is writing, or dancing or performance is you make something and then you build on it. You make a gesture and then you build on it. I need to get started and just do it. I need to get a mass of words down on the paper like a hunk of clay and begin shaping them and building them. Then one thing leads to the other thing. The same thing happens in painting and drawing. With the drawing and painting I have to be careful that it doesn't get too busy. With the writing, I have to make sure that I have a theme and I am not too scrambled, but those are technical things.

E: So you structure your creativity in a creative manner?

S: I have to take the time to do it. I'll go in and out of painting for long periods of time and what I am amazed at is its . . . sometimes better than ever. What I have learned about it is I just don't worry about it if I haven't painted for two months.

E: Do you ever go through periods where you go through one type of thing at a time, like Picasso's blue period?

S: I get obsessed with it.

E: Sure, because you get obsessed with like painting for 10 months and then it might be clay and then writing?

S: Oh yes, I become infatuated with it and become deeply involved with it. Maybe that is why I am polygamous with my art!

E: I am exactly the same way! (Here we both laughed!)

S: It is the way it works. I become infatuated with something. It's intense and runs it course. I need projects. I am really happiest when I am working on two books at the same time . . . love it. When I can't get to one . . . I need to move between things. When I am really into a book that is how I get it done, I find time to write the book, my family complains. I am gone.

E: Well of course, it's another relationship. I understand that completely.

S: Yup, I'm gone.

E: So that's what you mean by the state of creation? When you zone off.

S: I view this as concentration not dissociative, it is what I choose to focus on at that particular moment.

Yes, focusing on a particular moment. In essence, that is all each of us can do. Focus on a particular task, be it art, music, dance, writing, or the like. I interviewed many art therapists, among them, **Bruce Moon, Ph.D., A.T.R., B.C.**, author, poet, art therapist, and educator. Many of the artists that I interviewed independently said the same things. When talking to Bruce about his poetry, which is clearly a different art form than the theoretical books that he writes, and perhaps more akin to creating artworks, like Parker Palmer, he said the same thing:

Interview with Bruce Moon

B: Poetry is about living and dying, really. It is not an issue you resolve and get on with in your real life. You keep recycling, keep returning to it . . .

E: I understand that. When I write a poem, it takes a whole different flavor than writing a theoretical book. It is a different paradigm, I think.

B: In a way you are saying, if I go back to this image of the moment before creation, the poem stands closer to that point than a book does, five miles down the road from that.

I have just finished a manuscript and I have a stack of paper that is 3 1/2 inches high . . . but a poem, it holds you very close to the moment before creation . . . it is filled with life from that point of origin.

E: How do you feel when you are in that state? Do you have any sense of what your motives are?

B: As a man, I don't know how it feels to be pregnant, but . . . something like that.

E: I knew when I was pregnant . . . suddenly there was something that was not me, but of me.

B: Yes, it is like you said, of me, but not the same as me.

E: This is what I am talking about when I struggle with that dissociative or self-divide that I experience as an artist.

B: To me, in life it is to become the undivided self, to integrate, to come into coherence, with one's heart, to not live one way on the outside and contradicting some truth on the inside. To me, it has to do with an extended sense of self, that is a self that is not isolated, a self which is profoundly connected, it has to do with a self as being, rather than a self as doing.

E: I know that I am happiest, most connected, less worried, least anxious and most alive, when I am in that true self-state. There is nothing else like it for me. Nothing else takes me to that place. For me, the struggle is how to keep that balance operational. There are some people who live there all the time–Dali Lama, for example. But I get to it most often through my art, whatever form it is taking. So that is why I feel somehow dissociated, because I have to split off.

B: It is truly interesting to think about. When I think to put the first word on the paper, it is hard to find the next 200,000, knowing that there will be so many rejects in the line of the keepers. Some days, I feel like the world's worst writer, but still I am going to get up the next day and do it again.

E: So, you have those feelings.

B: Absolutely. And it takes ego to do the principal work (performance art) and get in front of audiences. Somebody says, "Well, this sucks!" and it takes "ego" not to collapse under the weight of that . . . so it is doing this amazing dance, a kind of tools of "selfhood." This is where we need the "undifferentiated self" that has its roots, deep . . . primordial life from which you draw creativity and life-giving . . . that bastard in the audience.
   I think of it as a myth. How was it before we achieved consciousness? Your whole thesis, in a way, is: "How can we live with a foot in both worlds? How can we have one foot in the Garden of Eden in a kind of primordial soup and maintain the playfulness of that?

E: Maybe that is it, the great attraction. Maybe when we are in that state of *elemental play*, that creative state that reminds us of our archetypal roots, maybe that is why it is so important for us to gravitate back and forth between both places.

B: I think so, it is in our backbones.

   Our backbones. Yes, ingrained into our consciousness. And as I stated earlier transmitted into our neuroepidural junctions (NEJ's). The collective unconscious. Perhaps this is why we have this biological urge to create, make art, and communicate through language, music, and the written word.

Interview with Valerie Appleton

Valerie Appleton, Ed.D., A.T.R., M.F.C., N.C.C. author, art therapist, poet, and artist, was the next interviewee. Like Moon, she also resonated with poetry as the writing link that informed her:

V: For me, writing poetry, keeping it in a journal, is probably the closest link I have with my own creative processes of art making. The link or information . . . is more metaphoric. In my scholarly writing, I . . . articulate what my identity is.

E: Can you tell me more about what that means for you?

V: I see myself as a counselor and art therapist. I teach students in a counselor program and I am really interested in the standards of how we teach that microskill . . . working in relationship with clients. We see them as experts about their situation and their heart is the modality . . . because it provides us with the . . . quickest method . . . and expertise of wellness that is in that client.

E: Does it do that for you when you are in the mode of doing your own artwork?

V: As an artist it absolutely does. When I paint, I am involved in this. I am in a very transient process where I am really lost in the experience of light and color. The color that drops into pigmentation . . . I go deeper into some stream of loneliness, and I can lose time, stay up later at night, see the sun rising and not knowing the time has come, gone. When I get to the end of the product . . . I do not particularly recognize that I have painted it, and yet I know it is a projection of me.

E: Could you describe how you separate and then reintegrate into that person you become?

V: The first thing that came into my mind is what the Bushmen of Kalahari say about teaching my students: There is a dream dreaming us. What I experience is an active awake state. But it is though a dream is dreaming me and I am not the dreamer anymore. It is a sort of change in the locus of control. This really speaks of the dissociation that can happen. For me dissociation rather than being pathological is a source place of generative place which I need to go back to, to stay home and stay balanced well.

E: Can you say more about the generative process and how it controls you?

V: It guides me and directs me . . . The voice of my father, for example, speaking to me about how the color is perceived and how you use it compositionally. Things like that. If I listen to that voice too much, the full surrendering to what is the really spontaneous flow of this process is . . . well, I have to stop, maybe listen to perhaps a critical voice that is observing the process. But I have to really surrender to the process that leads me forward, that is true process. There is no fear for me. There is nothing pathological or strange. This is why I described it as "delight"; the way the dissociation can happen is because of trust. I have some trust of the media as another that I am having a relationship with, that I am engaged with, that I am having a dialogue with or a dance with.

E: I am wondering about what you meant when you said, "it is a sense of delight." Do you have any sense of it being something you do not connect with very often except when you are in this creative state?

V: It is a state that is given spontaneously to my life, in happy little moments, like encounters with people. Usually, they are visual things that happen in some compound of time that I cannot control. It sort of happens on its own accord. It is the same process with media. The media has its own way of being and our manipulating and responding to it at the same time. Image results from it, symbols that are surprising which move me.

Like McNiff, Appleton described the creative process as a trust of the media. Moreover, she, too, described the process as "another" with whom she was having a "relationship." Each time I heard this, it resonated profoundly in me. When I am in the creative state, be it non-fiction writing, fiction writing, poetry, or making art, I am truly in relation with the other. I often joked repeatedly to my friends and colleagues that if I could sleep with my work that I would be the happiest person in the world. Perhaps it is because of the flow that accompanies this healthy, dissociative trance state. I do know that when I am in that state, I surrender to its mission. I don't contend with it, war with it, or even question the process. I just give into it, happily, in the same way that an infant suckles at a mother's breast. And maybe, just maybe, therein lies the attraction for me: I have always said that the only thing I feel I can truly rely on in this world is my work, *because* it has always been there for me. It is self-sustaining, life enhancing, and all giving. No human or animal relationship has been able to offer me anything like it and perhaps that is because it comes from within. The old adage of art therapists,' "draw from within," is a wellspring of information on the trajectory towards wellness.

The next interview is with **Gail Bellamy**, journalist, noted author and poet. Among her accomplishments, she has written a book called *Design Spirits*, which focuses on restaurants, bars, pubs and techno-clubs. Gail is also a dining columnist for *American,* a contributing food writer for *Cleveland Free Times,* a weekly alternative newspaper, and a contributing restaurant editor for *Table Wear Today* magazine. She has contributed to many books and her poetry has appeared in about 50 publications, including *Cosmopolitan, Rolling Stone,* and many literary and academic journals.

Interview with Gail Bellamy

E: Besides the fact that you also write poetry, do you play an instrument or practice another kind of art form? Would you consider yourself an artist in other fashions as well?

G: I play the violin and viola. I would not consider myself an artist at the violin, however, I would consider myself proficient.

E: How does language, or in your case the written word, inform for you cognition, thought, developmental creativity and discovery in you as a person?

G: Since language is the thing, literally and figuratively that speaks to me, other peoples words and writings give me ideas and insight. Sometimes, something that someone says or writes would give me an idea for something I am writing, not because of what they wrote or said but because of the images they chose. In journalism for example, many people can go to the same event, be given the same assignment, go to this concert and by ten o'clock tonight turn in a 500 word synopsis of what you have experienced for our readership. In my mind, I have never felt competitive with other writers because each of us will filter that experience through our own previous experience, own abilities, own knowledge, own intuition and what we form based on what we experience will be totally different. There will be as many different takes on that concert, as many 500 word synopsis as there are people in that room who had that same assignment.

E: I found intriguing that you said sometimes the images from what somebody says or the words that you read, create a spark for you or even an image for you, much the same way a landscape or an apple might create that type of imagery for me and then fuel my creativity. Is that what happens?

F: Yes. I am talking about choosing sometimes a word or a phrase or an observation of someone. You have to remember: out of the whole universe of things to say at a particular moment or in a particular written piece, somebody has chosen that for a reason, and besides, sometimes that wording . . . reaches out and touches a reader. You can also look one step beyond it and say how odd, that they are sitting there on the hill and looking at this and hearing that and yet they only wrote about the scene . . . Often, I give myself an assignment beyond the assignment of my job.

E: Based on your book, *Design Spirits,* the interior design aspect of your career, clearly I consider you an artist. Do you consider yourself an artist regarding what you wrote about those places?

G: I don't consider myself an "artist." I make jewelry, crafts, not art. I do things out of antique buttons that I have inherited, grandmothers and my great aunt, and a lot of them are just really weird and exotic things, but I consider that craft, not art. But I have sold them at boutiques and shops and just as an individual at different art sales. Again I would never be nervy enough to say that is art, but to me it is not.

E: Then, your primary art form that gives you your edge of creativity is words?

G: Absolutely.

E: Do you consider your poetry and your short stories an art form, which is a side off of the journalism?

G: I think that I have ample opportunity to interject a little bit of poetry into the things that I write journalistically. I would say that I definitely do that in design writing. Definitely, I try to do that in my book. I would say that every design write-up that I did, every synopsis of a project in that book had what I would consider a little line of poetry or a poetic image. And I do try and do that when I am writing about table setting or interior designing because it is a tribute to the people who have created something and you are writing about beauty that they created in their work. And so it is, I consider a way of trying to honor them.

E: Do you have any sense of how words make you connect you as a human being from one experience to the next? Do you have any sense on how it informs parts of you as a human being even in terms of physical senses?

G: Certainly, first of all, in writing it, an expression of the way you have filtered experience through your consciousness, or a way you have filtered emotions through your own consciousness and then the way you choose to express them to the world. In the cooking world, or in a broth, maybe our own minds are kind of this boiling all these things together in a big stew pot.

And then the cheese cloth or strainer that we pour it through is our own mind as a writer and then what you allow to come through is the broth or the expression or something that you present to the outside world, that is kind of how it works . . . I did a poem based on musical, physical feelings that were evoked by musical expressions or emotions that we had to music and how it would make you feel physically if you tried to express it to someone who had not heard it. For example, some of Bach's double violin concerto always reminds me of walking into a busy post office, all this input of people walking around and all these wonderful things and colors and then you are kind of scuffling your way to the front of the line. There is a little scuffling feeling that it evokes in me. Theses are the kinds of things that I am talking about. It is something that someone else triggers.

E: Because you are also musically inclined, is there ever a time where you have to turn off the music because the topic is such that you need full concentration of the written word coming than any other external stimulus?

G: No, when I have full concentration I am totally oblivious to people and music around me. I can be working on something in a really concentrated way and I can look at the clock and it will be four hours later. A lot of people say they need quiet to write or I can't write this article by my deadline and you're out in the hall talking too loud. I don't have that problem. When I am concentrating I concentrate in my own mind and so I am not aware of distractions. I guess the closest thing you could liken it to would be a working meditative state, because that is the level that I am working on. Some things that I am doing I consider exotic and free flight, and I can do whatever I want and its fun.

E: I am finding that everyone I have been interviewing describes it the same way, so it makes me feel that I am not off base by calling it *elemental play*, but nobody came right down and called it enjoyment the way you did, which I found very interesting. What I am finding is that a lot of people are saying the same things about creativity and what it evokes in them. So I am beginning to see a blanket woven on a similar point, that makes us all somewhat artistic in whatever way you want to call it. One of the things that I found about language is that sometimes words fall on a linear stage and it is flat but other times when you say things in a certain way and use words in a certain way ideas are born and they are enacted. All kinds of truths unfold for you that would not have been there otherwise. And I think that is somewhat of what you are talking about where it becomes sort of a primal pump.

G: Absolutely. It would be interesting to know if people who were self-made and self-taught artists, who had to nurture themselves, also had that area where they are also good in another art. I wonder if it is something that is just leisure time and opportunity and the nurturing given to you.

Naturally, Gail's last pondering gave me pause and rocked me to my senses. We dialogued more about this point before completing the interview. It was as if the people I had chosen to interview were wondering about some similarity. Was it a predisposition to creativity? A genetic link? Or was it in fact environmentally triggered? Did it have to be either/or? Could it be both/and? Talking about genetics led me to interview **David Henley, Ph.D., A.T.R.**, an art therapist who has written extensively about genetic linking to creativity. David is an art therapist, artist, poet, author, and educator.

Interview with David Henley

E: Recently I have discovered that my arts intertwine so I am asking you, how does your art inform your cognition, thought, language, and inquiry, if at all, and make them what they are?

D: It has to be the whole sensory apparatus. It is a fundamental way of making art that stays unconscious. You stay a stranger to it almost.

E: Bruce Moon talked about that when he said he felt like an "imageorator" as well as the aspect of "creative immersion." I talk about it as the concept of *elemental play*.

D: I keep it distant from me. I have no need for insight. It becomes a labor and as a labor it requires all these faculties that Edith (Kramer) talks about. She really represents all the original ideas. I just have applied all her ideas in different ways . . . the idea of having one's own art remaining distinct from the therapeutic process. I have created and crafted but I dip. I do this primary process dipping. They don't like to call it regressing anymore. The psychiatric gurus have decided that regression in service of the ego is not the right term. But this dipping is sort of an intentional retrieval. It drives the higher order faculties. It drives us, executes it. But it is very much a stranger to me.

E: So if it is a stranger to you, how do you feel if you part with it or don't you? Do you ever attempt to sell it, keep it, or do you give it away?

D: I make very few works that distinguishes me from someone like Bruce (Moon) who has recently made like 300 paintings. I make very few pieces. I rarely talk about it. Right now I am grinding lead paint off of revolutionary war ceilings. But I don't differentiate that from going to the studio.

E: I don't either.

D: See that's the thing, people who feel that their art is a way of problem-solving the psychodynamic issues . . . so many art therapists merge with their artist-selves. The aesthetic becomes saccharine-like. It is a very different kind of approach . . . If you don't define a line between art and art therapy, you're no longer doing either. Some are making the case that art therapy should be boundless (that is making art alongside others). That is so far away from what I do. Providing the art materials, that is the artist therapy approach.

E: Do you go through writing modes like Picasso's blue period of ten years?

D: Well, yes, but that is because it sometime takes that long to become competent at these things.

E: Maybe. I never thought of it from a developmental perspective.

D: I have an eye so I can translate images. The art therapist as critic is another aspect that we need to saddle up to because of the soul element. Trying to stay with the formal elements . . . when I interpret art, I never have to go into the symbolic meaning of the thing. It's purely manifest, it's there already. You just have to be trained to see it. Anybody can do it once they are trained to do it.

Let me give you an example: I had this head injury guy and in rehab' (in the late '70s) they didn't want any art therapy. They wanted no emotions because that would inhibit their cognitive therapy and motivation to supposedly progress. He placed this oblong, brown shape in the middle of the page and immediately became troubled because it so resembled a freshly dug grave. But verbally, he called it a mud pond. He next asked my opinion about how to make the composition more pleasing. After talking with him, he came up with the idea of rocks bordering the pond. But he placed in only one stone that clearly looked like a headstone and again he looked at it. I witnessed his psyche as he struggled with it. At the same time, I got him to look at that very thing that was popping up. And the neuropsychologist observed this whole session and it educated him to understand how people are constantly emoting and problem-solving simultaneously. That is the work that we do.

The importance of Kramer is art and for me it has never been exclusive. For me, it is not. I can spend long periods of time grinding the ceilings of revolutionary art and writing. I consider art to be a part of manual labor.

One of the most important messages I received from Edith Kramer was to never forget the importance and place of art in matters of the heart. "Ever art," Edith used to write on her communications after my graduation. I saved those notes and have invested their meaning and importance into my work for over 20 years. I am suggesting a return to an artistic core. In it is the humanity of our struggle as art therapists, but also the care for our own soul and that of our patients.

This mystery of what drives us to make art, what informs our cognition and thought processes, what fuels that creative spirit has been touched on above. For me, it is clear that I must create. It is akin to the endorphin release when I physically work out. I make art, I write, I play because I have to.

Some search endlessly for a soul mate, like the circular protagonist in Shel Silverstein's *The Missing Piece*. But I have found my missing piece: for me it is the self-soothing, auto-stimulating aspect of my creative psyche, the partner that never lets me down. For me, it is my art. And while I am not suggesting that one's art need be the only relationship, I am proposing that connection to one's internal creativity can foster wellness and self-transformation. Honing in on that instinctive, creative drive offers a sense of purpose and well-being. And that secondary gain might just lead one toward authentic behavior and in fact improve one's capacity for relationship. I know it has for me.

Vocatus atque no vocatus Deus aderit.
(Translation: Invoked or not invoked, God well be present)

C. G. JUNG

Chapter 7

CONCLUSIONS

A rt is language, albeit visual. For me, its vocabulary constitutes inner dialogue. While it is unclear whether the visual or literal image occurs first, what is transparent is its impact and effect. I still question how this dialogue occurs: that is, which comes first, the art or the words. Their interconnectedness, however, is what intrigues me. These inner dialogues come in varied fashion from artistic images (e.g., poetry, short stories, fiction, creative nonfiction, music, dance, dreams, etc.). Of utmost importance is receptivity to these messages. When I am open to the meaning behind these directives, I find they have direction and bearing in my life and work.

My graduate students have asked me why I designed the BATA (Belief Art Therapy Assessment) in my last book, *Spiritual Art Therapy: An Alternate Path.* The entire notion came from a dream that I had the night before I was to teach my first preschool, Sunday school class. I had spent numerous hours attempting to prepare for that day and when I received the dream, a directive to explore children's impressions about "what God **meant** to them," I scrapped my entire lesson plan. I still remember swinging my legs over the side of the bed and saying out loud, "What the Hell was that all about?" The message had been quite explicit in asking the children to draw, paint or sculpt what it was that God "**meant**" to them. I felt compelled to follow this dream and explore it with children, adults, clergy, and eventually with the patients with whom I worked. The dream certainly had been propelled by what I had been currently investigating, but the message in the dream ignited the pyre into activity. I could have simply ignored the dream and written off its message. But, this was no ordinary dream. At that time, I hadn't really ingested the idea of God coming into "particularity" through each of us. But years later, the idea of a Higher Being (name it what you will) coming into/being a part of all energy certainly makes perfect sense to me and copious others. According to Myss (1996):

> This shift from religion to spirituality is not simply a cultural trend. It is an archetypal reorganization of our planetary community, which now has access to the universal truths available through symbolic sight. Symbolic sight includes a sixth sense of intuition, which senses the connections among all liv-

171

ing energy. . . It seems as though humanity is "under orders" to mature spirituality to a level of holistic sight and service, and any number of paths of service to fulfill those orders that have opened up to us. (pp. 270–271)

Pathways. Ways of coming into particularity. Symbolic sight. Messages take on various forms disguised in all kinds of interchange with the energy that surrounds us. For me, these often come in what Myss might describe as being "under order." Such as the case of the dream that led me to the direction of my last book.

What has become clear to me is that I seem to be here in this time and in this life for some purpose, perhaps greater than I can fathom. While I often read the news and am aware of the atrocities around me, occasionally I ask myself why I have been so blessed. Sure, looking at my genogram the reader might argue that last statement, but the truth of the matter is that all my life experiences, my pain, pleasure and sufferings, have made me the person that I am. And I bring all that perceptiveness to my work as an artist/therapist/clinician. All of that energy informs my artistic work and the work that I do with my clients. To ignore that individuality, that gift that each of us has, is a mistake. We cannot help bringing our conscious self to our work. It matters not if one is a therapist, business executive, farmer, grocery checker, or surgeon. We bring our issues and ourselves to our work no matter how hard we try and filter them out. While I dissociate when donning the protective veneer of the "therapist," most of the time, I am constantly bringing my self to work. If I am truly working on my self in an authentic manner, then this dissociative state becomes *elemental play* and thus I allow myself to connect with the patient as another human being on the trajectory towards wellness.

I was instructed to be a "neutral" albeit impartial therapist. I was mentored in all the right principles like "don't wear seductive clothing," "match the client at his/her level," and "attend to the patient's needs and not your own." And while all that is fine, clear and correct advice, the maxim which suggests leaving oneself "out of the therapy" is sound counsel but misguided in practice. Don't misunderstand. I am not suggesting that one spill one's history to a client or announce in session what troubles one is having in his/her family of origin. Rather I am suggesting offering information where it fits.

While training under a certified AAMFT (American Association of Marriage and Family Therapy) clinician, I have been taught to pay attention to the light bulbs that periodically go off in my head. I have been instructed to adjust these signs to the needs of the client. For example, in working with children of manic-depressive parents, I have indeed shared my background, my childhood experiences, and even my fears about growing up only to possibly inherit the disease. Sharing the history behind my mother's illness has not contaminated the session but rather enhanced trust and created a mutual vulnerability that indeed makes me human. Indeed, such therapeutic admission has bridged and connected me to my patients. Moreover, it offers a role model of authenticity. After all, if we are expecting our clients to face their demons, what better model than to show them the way?

I have chosen this model knowing in my heart that it is grounded in integrity and constructed on the maxim that you can*not* take your patients any further than you have gone yourself. Its railway leads to transformation of self. And so by default, the primary process gain that informs the therapist (via authentic communication and embracing one's art as a vehicle of communication) bears secondary gains: the client seems to get better. It is that simple. The patients with whom I have worked have improved by this method. While it may not be a panacea, gains seem to be made and changes, be they small or significant, occur. I am convinced it is because I allow for this mix of energy, am open to its power, and share that wonderment with my patients. I welcome it, be it dark and frightening or open and clearing. In doing so, I model a transformative process that states: be present, be open, invite change.

In this book, I have postulated the inherent possibilities in using myself as a model for transformation when working with emotionally disturbed patients as well as within the framework of my own ministry. What I have concluded again and again is the importance of creation or *elemental play*. Whether artistic endeavors rub off on myself, my patients, or the students whom I train, the outcome seems to be the same. Metaphorically, I see this application as equivalent to throwing a small pebble into a large body of water. The pebble breaks the surface of the water, spreads out into concentric circles, and perpetually creates energy anew as it washes up against another life form.

In viewing myself as this permeable entity, I see my life, its direction, and its process as a gift. I truly feel that every being (whether animate or inanimate) offers a gift. As a result, I perceive every interaction with each life form as a source of energy. My subjective experience with all matter (whether negative or positive) causes me to constantly change and grow. While intrinsically I will always be the same person, I seem to be constantly changing. As a result, the state of inertia has little meaning for me. Instead, I view this path as a lifelong trajectory towards wellness. It is, perforce, what keeps me alive, enabling me to explore life with childlike wonder while simultaneously understanding it from previous life experiences.

As a result, I embrace change, including that which I cannot control. I used to be quite affected by the inequities of the world and the conditions that many people face on a daily basis. While the horrid condition and squalor of others' plights still concern me, I have come to view these contrasts to my life experience quite differently. Presently, the sordid injustice of the world's state still appalls me yet the outcome seems to have changed. So the reader will not misunderstand me, I want to underscore my position: this is *not* about indifference on my part. Rather it is acceptance, acceptance of a greater wisdom than mine, acceptance of my own impermanence and that around me, acceptance of my own condition. This does not mean that I am apathetic or unconcerned with activist positioning.

Instead, it is merely reception to the universe. I do what I can. I have my causes, my beliefs, my attempts (no matter how small) to make the world a better, safer, and more compassionate place. But the egocentric position of "changing" the world is not one to which I ascribe. I recognize the fact that my *existence* alone changes the world and therefore influences its outcome. But I am no more than a small bug, or as I have stated before, a spoke on the great cogwheel of life. I have had good fortune in my life but I by no means interpret that as ownership. In other words, I have embraced the permanence in impermanence.

While the idea of impermanence may seem both temporal and transitory, it is. But then again, our stay on this planet, in this lifetime, is in fact just that: no more than an interim visa until the next plane. It's really like operating from the position of tourism: passing through life as a well-seasoned traveler, one accepts that the stay is temporary and bears no more than a green card visa for work. You see, while technology keeps chipping away at the possibility of creating human immortality and cloning (a thought that makes me shudder), I look forward to the inevitable separation from this transient existence. I just see it as a point on the trajectory. I love life and live it to the hilt and that is why if it ended for me tomorrow, I would just as readily relinquish it to the next stage. I'm not suggesting that I want to suffer. I don't. I have no desire for my life to end tragically and/or be altered from the current state that I enjoy. However, if my life were to end, then that in itself is part of the greater picture.

This concept reminds me of Cathy Moon's beautiful performance art piece, "*Making Art from Bits and Pieces of Lives Discarded*," at the 28th Annual American Art Therapy Association in Milwaukee, Wisconsin in 1997. In her moving performance about another art therapist's untimely death, (her best friend, Deb DeBrular), Cathy reiterated the pain which she experienced both personally and that which she felt in the work with her patients. As she smacked a small rock against another rock, she sang, "Bone chip against bone chip against bone chip against bone chip. . .." I love Cathy. I hated seeing her in such pain over the loss of her closest friend. But I also found comfort in her visual and artistic suffering and the way in which she moved these feelings up and out. Having experienced so much loss in my personal life, I identified with her feelings, wept for her pain, and loved her for authentically sharing her beliefs and mourning with a larger audience while simultaneously connecting it to patient issues. It was at once brave, personal and archetypal. For as Cathy so eloquently articulated in her lines, "Bone chip against bone chip against bone chip . . .," the message became transparent: this is what we do. It is painful and necessary work.

Beginning with losses reconnects patients to their very origin of dis-ease (e.g., symptomatic discomfort) and sets the stage for inclusion of the spiritual dimension. If the therapist skips over these elements too quickly, then the work is not only hampered but also spiritual evolution is impeded (Horovitz-Darby, 1994.) As Moore suggests, the work of therapists would change radically "if we thought about it as ongoing care rather than a quest for a cure" (1992, p. 19).

While mourning is restoration in and of itself, leveling the pain attached to loss is tantamount to all the issues and symptoms which so cleverly arise from this persistent grasp. Focusing on mourning and loss issues cannot be ignored and *must* be the principal step towards recovery (Horovitz-Darby, 1994). Without this primacy, there may be change but not resolution, evolution or *soulution.* Instead, the symptoms will rear their ugly little heads again and again until these losses are aired, examined, and most importantly accepted. It is then and only then that the real work can begin.

A Promising Future

I see broad application for the work that we do as art therapists. It can be as immediate as changing one person's life (as I outlined in Chapters 2, 3, and 4) and as far reaching as transforming the therapist (Chapter 1). The practice of using individual and family therapy approaches is commonplace in the literature. Art Therapy's inherent application when applied to the clinician has not been so loudly pronounced. But our world is changing and while working within a personal framework (that is one on one, small groups or with families) is the "meat and potatoes" (so to speak) of our industry, I see many other applications for art therapy's inherent future.

Our world is complex, fast paced, and often overwhelming. Computers are ubiquitous. I come from the last generation where books and radio preceded television. That is, I remember when my grandmother got her first black and white (yes, black and white!) television. And, I am only 46. Much has transpired in my childhood. Color television has replaced the black and white versions, calculators (once prohibitively expensive in the early 1970s) are as commonplace as cereal. And computers (heretofore reserved for scientists) are accessible to the general public for worldwide application and exchange.

I love how humanity advances and continues to grow. I don't view computers as monsters. I see them as tools. While they are a far cry from the prehistoric wheel, they are tools nonetheless. From cloning to information exchange, they can have both disastrous and miraculous implications.

Anything in the wrong hands can have cataclysmic bearing. But with fore-thought, imagination and unheralded creativity, computers can have far-reaching potential.

Forensic Implications

I envision a day when police officers may work hand and hand with art therapists. It is quite possible right now for the following anecdote to occur: A young child, traumatized by a recent nodal event (such as a bombing, rape, or murder) is brought into a police station. Perhaps she is electively mute. No one can get through to her. A well-intentioned officer offers the young child a piece of paper, some art materials and watches as she creates. The officer is amazed at the child's sense of calm or anxiety (whichever the case may be). The child still does not talk, somewhat catatonic in her ability to verbalize. The work is scanned into a computer, transformed into a "JPEG, BMP, or TIF file" and then instantly e-mailed to me. I open it up with a request from a far-off place to view this work and offer feedback to the officer in this town of let's say, East Cupcake. While I could offer an analyt-ic take, a mental status, a diagnostic indicator of what I perceive to be occur-ring (and some would call that 'imagicide'), I just might be able to offer infor-mation that the officer missed and in this consultation, aid the small child who didn't have access to an art therapist clinician. This work is not far-off and it is not fiction. I am presently exploring this modality in my work.

Another scenario: A young child is disinterested in using traditional art materials; instead his ADHD (Attention Deficit Hyperactivity Disorder) causes him to be impulsive and chaotic. But he *loves* computers. This child hates himself, his face and his image because of horrific physical abuse. He has been burned over 75 percent of his body and face. Others shun him and consider him "ugly." He views himself the same way.

We take a digital camera and I snap pictures of him which he then down-loads into the computer. He opens up these images in the software, Photoshop. He manipulates, disguises, and alters the image until the self-por-trait is to his liking. He prints it out on a sheet of acetate. The acetate is then placed on an overhead projector. The image is projected onto a blank can-vas. He outlines the image. He begins a revisioning of himself and thereby works on his self-image and the pain attached to the loss of self as he once knew it. Fiction? No, application.

We can be as far-reaching as we dare. We can choose to use that which sur-rounds us in unparalleled connection. The world is our canvas.

My interest in implementing the concepts of invoking a studio art therapy approach, *elemental play* and *soulution* has had far-reaching application. This is not so new. Edith Kramer (1958) talked about this in her book on working with the Wiltwick School for Boys. We just seem to be returning to the basics.

There seems to be a paradigm shift afoot, at least in this decade. Scores of New Age titles have appeared on the horizon and a multitude of interest seems to be growing in transformation of the mind/body/spirit continuum. While I have been driven by this quest since at least eight years of age, I find small comfort in finally connecting with other thinkers who share my passion for such direction (Horovitz-Darby, 1994).

Oddly enough, this paradigm shift seems to be shaking up every strata of society: such ideas are even emerging in business and technology. (Heermann, 1997) In a recent discussion with a computer scientist who specializes in digital imaging, Matraszek (1997) discussed the importance of technology receiving cues from the environment and stated that "the flowing of energy from the earth is the language of primordial wisdom." This statement connects strongly to Levinthal's (1988) view of the brain as "an archeological dig, where the strata of past civilizations extend downward to greater and greater antiquity."

Levinthal (1988) suggested that we are ineptly named *Homo Sapiens* and should instead be called *Homo Ludens* (or the one who plays). Perhaps creativity lies at the core of this dilemma. Other theorists such as Csikszentmihalyi (1996) have proposed invoking creativity in order to propel humankind towards an evolutionary pathway.

Participating in a universal construct that is greater than we are is fundamental in enlisting wellness. It enfolds humility and keeps lofty, self-serving ideas at bay. In this, there is a sense of innocence and childlike naiveté. Embracing humility reminds me of the art of learning a foreign language. Opening oneself to learning another language is a humbling experience and one that I very much enjoy. Perhaps this is why I am so terribly attracted to other languages: it opens me to pure cognition and thought processes from a childlike base. It is impossible to learn a language from an adult perspective. Instead, connecting language to one's primary language base is a bit like mixing paint for the very first time. A good base of Latin (for example) is invaluable for the medical student. The same thing is true for the language of art and the art therapist. In order to truly understand other human beings and what the art work represents for each individual, we must start with ourselves: looking within and knowing the art materials: that is ingesting its language and its message. I find this just as important as learning to be a therapist by being in therapy. It is not so much because of the "wounded healer" position so much as knowing what it is like to be on the hot seat. Again, the maxim of not being able to go any further than you have gone yourself is applicable here. This is true for therapeutic investigation as well as exploration with the art materials. Each pathway leads to self-examination and self-process. It is true that the unexamined life is not worth living. While scrutiny may be painful, I find it to be both necessary and satisfying work.

On Finishing Touches and Living with the Art

For many months, as I was writing this book, I was attempting to finish an oil painting that began when I started this treatise. Months passed and several other works of art weaseled their way into the folds of these pages. But still one painting remained unfinished in my studio. I stared at it, put it aside, and often replaced it on my easel. Still, I would remove it and paint something else or create another sculpture. I couldn't bear to face this work. I avoided it steadfastly for over a year and yet, it haunted me.

Like a mandala, it presented itself full circle. While working on this painting, I had planned a trip to visit my mother. I started working on it right before I was to leave but left sufficient time for it to dry so that I could pack it in my suitcase and take it with me. After several aggravating days and meditative jaunts to the Atlantic Ocean, I decided to paint it one evening and enlisted my mother to purchase some large hothouse tomatoes to help me complete the painting. My mother, who had eaten tomatoes like an apple all of my life, had no tomatoes in her home when I arrived. I was perfectly shocked to discover this. I needed to add a tomato to the painting.

Growing up, I couldn't stand the sound that my mother made when she ate tomatoes. It bothered me so much that it wasn't until my early 40s that I could actually eat one. This same sound also plagued my sister and brother, although they weren't so obsessed with the tomato as I. (They had been eating them for years while I was still steadfastly avoiding the "love fruit.") But the tomato plagued me; I spent months ruminating about its importance in my personal therapy, discussing its impact on me with my siblings and my very close friends. Some friends implored me to think of a word connected to the sound that I recalled (and/or from which I recoiled). But I was blocked and knew that for me the answer would be revealed in working through the process with art. Of interest is that I still avoided the pain connected to this memory by placing my sister in the painting instead of me. (Perhaps this offered me sufficient distance.)

Nevertheless, I decided to enlist my good friend and colleague, art historian, Dr. Roger Adams, for his interpretation of the above painting, "To'Maida." Roger was more than happy to comply since he was aware that his previous comments (as outlined in Figure 5 in Chapter 1) had contributed to a breakthrough in my writing. So the fateful evening of this year's faculty show, I sauntered up to Roger and asked him once again to look at the work with me and offer his input. After studying the work for some time, he turned to me and uttered the following words: "That's a pretty good lookin' tomato". He smiled wryly as he saw the wheels turning inside my head and walked away.

Figure 61. *Tò'Maida.* Oil, 16 in. x 20 in.

It is interesting that the vegetable tomato is known as the "love fruit." Considering how much I struggled with lack of mothering as a child, it seems even more ironic to me that I struggled so ardently with the sounds, which emanated from my mother's pleasure when eating this fruit. Once again, I was rocked back to a description that I had written of my mother in the novel that I am still writing:

> Suddenly, Ellen spied the familiar Electra 225 Buick approaching the camp director's residential quarters. Oddly enough, David looked somewhat worn. Although he had always looked ten years younger than his true age, today his face revealed a downhearted, morose caliber. His skin sallowed. Yet as he advanced toward the children, he momentarily brightened. Then Maida stepped out of the car. David froze. Maida sauntered forth, a charade of mismatched, fashion statements from the Whore Regime. Maida's dress was just a tad too tight, the buttons undone just low enough to entice onlookers to admire her cleavage and voluptuous breasts. Her bra was so ill-fitted that when she bent over, her bronze-colored nipples peeked out of the very tip of her brassiere. Maida's dress was oh-so-tight emphasizing her large, inviting but-

tocks and the slit at the dress base practically begged for admission. Her fuck-
me pumps elevated her shapely calves, accentuated by her seamed stockings.
The black, snake-like line twisted endlessly up her thighs. Her facial lips were
overwhelmingly large, accentuated by the fire engine, red lipstick that adorned
them. Maida's dark, brown eyes seemed at once clouded and simultaneously
excessive. Her obviously bleached, blonde hair was coifed in a 1950s flip that
somehow contorted, suggesting Maida's state of mind.

It was intriguing to recall that passage in my novel, *"Lithium for Lunch,"*
and equate it to the memories of my mother's seductive behavior. Again,
while the above passage from the novel is **inexactly** based on my childhood
memories, the comment made by Roger about the painting, "a pretty good
lookin' tomato," finally hit home: I had equated the sound that my mother
made with her seductive quality when in the throes of her mania. My mother's direct contact with the viewer and the baby's eye on the tomato underscored how traumatized I was by her erratic behavior. The innocent comment made by Roger uncovered this for me. Finally, I understood the repul-
sion that I had experienced from the tomato. This sound reiterated in my
ears because of my associations to my mother's Jezebel qualities. While I
understood (intellectually) that seductive, heightened sexual demeanor was
one of the behaviors attributed to manic-depression (Goodwin & Jamison,
1992), knowing this fact and connecting it to my abreaction was devoid of
meaning until I worked the process through in my art work.

Art is a powerful uptake. Shaun McNiff was quite right when he pre-
scribed "art as medicine" (McNiff, 1992). More importantly, in a recent conversation with my colleague, Dr. Valerie Appleton, we discussed the advan-
tage of "living with one's work." Beyond the struggle and medicinal qualities
connected to the process of creating artwork, another elemental feature is
simply living with the work. For months, I would bed down with my art and
awake the next day only to stare at the same unfinished canvas. Sittings with
that image for hours, days, and finally months contributed to a breakthrough
not only in my writing and art but also finally in my psyche.

While many have talked about the process of doing art, it is *both* meaningful and important to investigate the property of *living* with one's work.
Occupying the same space with the undertaking makes it a bedfellow in the
process of unraveling its personal relationship to the maker. I am quite certain that living with one's work can offer fruitful dialogue and inner meaning
to the creator. It really is no different than the composer who toils endlessly
on a composition, fine tuning the lyrical and musical quality until it has
orchestrated not only the maker but also in turn its audience. This process of
'art making the maker' holds rare insights for the creator and as in my case
has offered transformative, life-changing applications.

I have been advised by my well-meaning sister to never go to sleep in the same room as my laptop computer since for her, sleeping with the tool causes an abundance of energy that prevents her from accessing sleep. Other writers suggest never writing on Mondays. I have always written on Mondays and in fact have written two books primarily on this sacred writing day. I am of the opinion that there are no prescriptions for individual creativity. This life flow has to come from within. It is dictated from a well within each of us that defies boundary or description. What works for me may not be applicable for another. But I am convinced that truly living with one's work causes an entirely different result. Like the elephant in the room, it cannot be ignored. Its presence is both powerful and influential. I suggest that toiling in this manner can offer unprecedented insights for the maker and may possess even greater insights for working with one's patients.

Figure 62. *Babka Smietankowa.* Oil and mixed media on linen, 15 in. x 15 in.

In this final painting, "Babka Smietankowa" (Polish for sweet cupcake), the poem, *on winged ground* (recited at the 28th American Art Therapy Association Conference), preceded the painting. It is indeed rare for me to have a piece of writing influence my artwork. But this poem, which disguised metaphors of flight, love, and truth, was literally created while I was airborne. I wrote and rewrote *on winged ground* for over an hour until it finally felt right. When I finished the poem, I placed it into a handmade watercolor card and sent it off to the subject of this painting.

Upon my return home, the painting began. Soon after, I had to head off to the 28th American Art Therapy Association meeting. So I rolled up this linen napkin canvas (that had been my mother's), placed it in a cardboard tube, and packed it (along with oil paints, turpentine, and brushes) into my suitcase. Every night after the conference festivities had ended, I escaped to the solitude of my hotel room and painted into the night. By the third conference day, when it was time for my recitation at a Poetry Panel with David Henley, A.T.R., Bruce Moon, Ph.D., A.T.R., Cathy Moon, A.T.R., and Bob Schoenholtz, A.T.R., B.C., the "veins" of the painting were beginning to emanate from the face. (Of interest to me was that the last lines of the poem (which sparked the painting) were "we are veined possibilities").

While I normally never show a piece of artwork until it is completed, at the annual conference, I recited the poem with the linen canvas draped over the podium. The painting, which was still in progress, was just beginning to take on the "veined" qualities of the poem. I felt quite vulnerable, not only because I was reading highly personal poetry related to this art but because I was bearing a "work in progress." This in itself was quite unlike me. It told of risks to come: changes and "veined possibilities" that even I had not contemplated. Many of my colleagues really resonated with my poetry and risk-taking and heralded my forthright words and unbridled character. It felt so affirming to be appreciated for my venture.

My readings had not been cloaked in relation to my patients but instead, like all of my artworks, were drenched in personal meaning to my self. I was honored by the feedback. Somehow, I had spoken volumes to others and by sharing my current struggle as related to my artwork, I had somehow touched something in other artists.

I knew that in many respects my readings were very much "out on a limb." After all, this was a professional meeting, yet here I was sharing my most personal work with my colleagues. Finally, I knew that I was on the right track. For I had been acting out of center. I had been respecting others' intentions and people were responding to me *because* I was acting out of my center and *not* theirs. I had been engaged in speaking my truth. This authentic behavior was causing a shift in my artistic evolution and those around me. I had returned home to my most inner self, that peaceful sanctum which is my truth.

This virtue shapes life and love, rooting others in its pathway and it is authenticated from the heart. I have come to understand that I need to approach others as I engage myself: with honor, respect, sincerity, patience, trust, and love. It is more than the commandment "do unto others as you wish they do unto you." It is a way of life. Staying in this momentum is so very simple: it is learning to have heart, heart for those with whom we work and heart for ourselves. This is a very precious commodity, this life that we have been offered. It is in fact, a great gift. In my artwork, my teachings, and my work with clients, I have come to recognize this energy. Wisdom and transformation come from recognizing this force, honoring its intention, and speaking its truth. May you unfold and speak yours.

BIBLIOGRAPHY

Achterberg, J. (1985). *Imagery in healing: shamanism and modern medicine.* Boston: Shambala.

Allen, P. (1995a). Coyote comes in from the cold: the evolution of the open studio concept. *Arts in Psychotherapy.* Vol. 12: No. 3, pp. 161- 166.

Allen, P. (1995b). *Art as a way of knowing.* Boston: Shambala Press.

Alschuler, R. & Hattwick, H. (1947). *Painting & Personality.* Illinois: University of Chicago Press.

American Psychiatric Association. (1994). *Diagnostic and statistical manual of mental disorders,* fourth edition. Washington, D.C: American Psychiatric Association.

Assagioli, R. (1965) *Psychosynthesis.* New York: Viking.

Becker, R.O. (1985). *The body electric.* New York: Morrow.

Bergman, Z., Witzum, E., & Bergman, T. (1991). When words lose their power: Shiatsu as a strategic tool in psychotherapy. *Journal of Contemporary Psychotherapy,* Vol. 21, No. 1, pp. 5–23.

Bond, A.H. (1989). *Who killed Virginia Woolf, a psychobiography.* New York: Insight Books; Human Services Press.

Bowden, C.L. & McElroy, S.L. (1995) History of the development of Valproate for treatment of bipolar disorder. *Journal of Clinical Psychiatry,* Vol. 56 (Suppl. 3), 3-5.

Bruner, J. (1979). The conditions of creativity in *Consciousness: brain, states of awareness and mysticism.* ed. D. Goleman & R.J. Davidson, NY: Harper & Row, pp. 58–62 (quote on p. 58).

Buck, J.N. (1987). *The House-Tree-Person technique.* Revised Manual. CA: Western Psychological Services.

Burns, R.C. & Kaufman S.H. (1972). *Action styles and symbols in kinectic family drawings (KFD).* New York: Brunner/Mazel.

A course in miracles. (1992). 2nd rev. ed. Set of 3 vols., including text, teacher's manual, workbook, Found Inner Peace.

Cameron, J. (1992). *The artist's way.* New York: G.G. Putnam's Sons.

Campbell, J. (1974). *The mythic image.* New Jersey: Princeton University Press.

Chomsky, N. (1965). *Aspects of theory of syntax.* Cambridge, MA: MIT Press.

Csikszentmihalyi, M. (1993). *The evolving self, a psychology for the third millennium.* New York: Harper Perennial.

Csikszentmihalyi, M. (1996). The creative personality. *Psychology Today.* July/August, pp. 34–40.

Dissanayake, E. (1992). *Homo Aestheticus: Where art comes from and why.* New York: The Free Press.

English, O.S. (1949). Observation of trends in manic-depressive psychosis. *Psychiatry,* 12:125-134.

Ford, C. (1992). *Where the Healing Waters Meet.* New York: Station Hill Press.

Fraenkel, D. (1997). Personal Communication.

Frankel, V. (1984). *Man's search for meaning: an introduction to logotherapy* . New York: Simon and Schuster.

Friday, N. (1977). *My mother my self.*

Fromm-Reichmann, F. (1949). Intensive psychotherapy of manic-depressives. *Confina Neurologica,* 9: 158-165.

Gaskill, S. (1997). Keep art in the budget. *Democrat & Chronicle.* New York: Gannett Publications, July 11, 1997.

Gazzaniga, M. S. (1998). The split brain revisited. *Scientific American.* July, pp. 50-55.

Goodman, R. & Wilson, L. (1987). Establishing civil service job classifications for creative arts therapists in New York State. *Journal of Art Therapy.* October, Vol. 20, No. 1.

Goodwin, F.K. & Jamison, K.R. (1992). *Manic-depressive illness.* New York: Oxford.

Gray, E.S. (1998). Personal Communication.

Gutin, J.C. (1996). That fine madness. *Discover.* October, Vol. 17, Number 10, pp. 75-82.

Haley, J. (1986). *The power tactics of Jesus Christ and other essays.* New York: W.W. Norton & Company.

Hammer, E. (1990). *Reaching the affect/style in psychodynamic therapies.* New York: Aronson Inc.

Hammer, E. (1975). *The clinical application of projective drawing techniques,* fourth printing. Springfield, IL: Charles C Thomas.

Harvey, M.A. (1982). The influence and use of an interpreter for the deaf in family therapy. *American Annals of the Deaf,* 819-827.

Henley, D.R. (1992). *Exceptional children, exceptional art: teaching art to special needs.* Worcester, MA: Davis Publications, Inc.

Jamison, K.R. (1995). *The unquiet mind.* New York: Alfred Knopf.

Jones, D. (1999). Personal Communication.

Heermann, B. (1997). *Building team spirit.* New York: McGraw-Hill.

Horovitz, E.G. (1981). Art therapy in arrested development of a preschooler. *Arts in Psychotherapy,* an international journal, Vol. 8, No. 2, 119-126.

Horovitz, E.G. (1983). Preschool aged children: when art therapy becomes the modality of choice. *Arts in Psychotherapy,* Vol. 10, No. 2, 23-32.

Horovitz, E.G. (1988). Short term family art therapy: a case study Chapter 11 in *Two Decades of Excellence: A Foundation for the Future.* (Eds. Watson, D., Long, D., Taff-Watson, & Harvey, M.), Little Rock, AK: American Deafness and Rehabilitation Association (ADARA).

Horovitz-Darby, E.G. (1988). Art therapy assessment of a minimally language skilled deaf child. Proceedings from the 1988 University of California's Center on Deafness Conference: *Mental Health Assessment of Deaf Clients: Special Conditions.* Little Rock, AK: ADARA.

Horovitz-Darby, E.G. (1991). Family art therapy within a deaf system. *Arts in Psychotherapy,* Vol. 18, pp. 251-261.

Horovitz-Darby, E. G. (1992). Countertransference: implications in treatment and post-treatment. *Arts in Psychotherapy,* Vol. 19, pp. 379-389.

Horovitz-Darby, E.G. (1994). *Spiritual art therapy: an alternate path.* Springfield, IL: Charles C Thomas.

Horovitz, E.G. (1998). Book review for *Art and soul: an artistic psychology. Art Therapy.* Volume 15, No. 3.

Itten, J. (1974). *The Art of Color: The subjective experience and objective rationale of color.* New York: Van Nostrand Reinhold.

Jones, D. (1997). Personal Communication.

Kahn, D. (1990). The psychotherapy of mania. *Psychiatric clinics of North America.* June Vol. 13(2), 229-240.

Kramer, E. (1975). *Art as therapy with children.* New York: Schocken Books.

Kramer, E. (1981). Private Communications.

Levinthal, C. (1988). *Messengers of paradise: opiates and the brain the struggle over opium, rage, uncertainty and addiction.* New York: Anchor Books.

Lewin, B.D. (1951). *The psychoanalysis of human elation.* London: Hogarth Press.

Lowenfeld, V. & Brittain, W.L. (1975). *Creative and mental growth (6th Ed.).* New York: Macmillan.

Matrasek, T. (1997). Personal Communication.

Myss, C. (1996). *Anatomy of the Spirit.* New York: Harmony Books.

Naumburg, M. (1980). *Dynamically oriented art therapy: its principles and practices: illustrated with case studies.* Chicago, IL: Magnolia Street Publishers.

McNiff, S. (1995). Keeping the studio. *Arts in Psychotherapy.* Vol. 12, No. 3, pp. 179-183.

McNiff, S. (1992). *Art as medicine/creating therapy of the imagination.* MA: Shambala Press.

McNiff, S. (1998). *Art-based research.* England: Jessica Kingsley Publishers.

Moon, B.L. (1990). *Existential art therapy: the canvas mirror.* Springfield, IL: Charles C Thomas.

Moon, B.L. (1996). *Art and soul: An artistic psychology.* Springfield, IL: Charles C Thomas.

Moon, C. (1997). Making art from bits and pieces of lives discarded. *Proceeding of the 28th Annual American Art Therapy Association.* Milwaukee, WI.

Moustakas, C. (1994). *Being-in, being-for, being with.* New York: Aronson.

Nauman, E. (1995). *Poisons that heal.* AZ; Blue Turtle Publishing.

Negroponte, N. (1995). Being decimal. *Wired.* November, p. 252.

Noble, J.N. (1996). "Archaeologists in Australia find earliest signs of artistic behavior." *New York Times.* September 21, 1996.

Rennie, J. (1998). From the editors: all for one. *Scientific American.* p. 8.

Rubin, J.A. (1984). *The art of art therapy.* New York: Brunner/Mazel.

Sharma, V., Persad, E., Mazmanian. D. & Karunaratne, K. (1993). Treatment of rapid cycling bipolar disorder with combination therapy of Valproate and Lithium. *Canadian Journal of Psychiatry.* Mar Vol. 38 (2), 137-139.

Shoemaker, R. (1977). The significance of the first picture. *Proceedings from the 8th Annual American Art Therapy Association.* IL: AATA.

Silver, R.A. (1970). Art and the deaf. *Bulletin of Art Therapy.* Washington, D.C.: Ulman.

Silver, R.A. (1978). *Developing cognitive and creative skills through art.* Baltimore: University Park Press.

Silver, R.A. (1996). *The silver drawing test of cognition and emotion.* FL: Ablin Press.

Silver, R.D. (1976). *Shout in silence, visual arts and the deaf.* Rye, New York: Silver Publications.

Silverstein, S. (1976). *The missing piece.* New York: Harper Collins Publishers.

Sontag, S. (1995). *Illness as metaphor and AIDS and its metaphors.* Peter Smith Publishers.

Sweet, R.B. (1990). *Writing towards wisdom: the writer as shaman.* Carmichael, CA: Helios House.

Vygotsky, L.S. (1962). *Thought and language.* Cambridge, MA: MIT Press.

Waya, A.G. (1992). *Soul recovery and extraction.* AZ: Blue Turtle Publishing.

Woodcock, J. (1997). Personal Communication (8/26/97).

Woolf, L. (1964). *Beginning again: an autobiography of the years 1911-1918.* New York: Harcourt.

Woolf, V. (1929). *A room of one's own.* New York: Harcourt Brace.

AUTHOR INDEX

SUBJECT INDEX

191